CAPE SCOTT

AND THE

NORTH COAST TRAIL

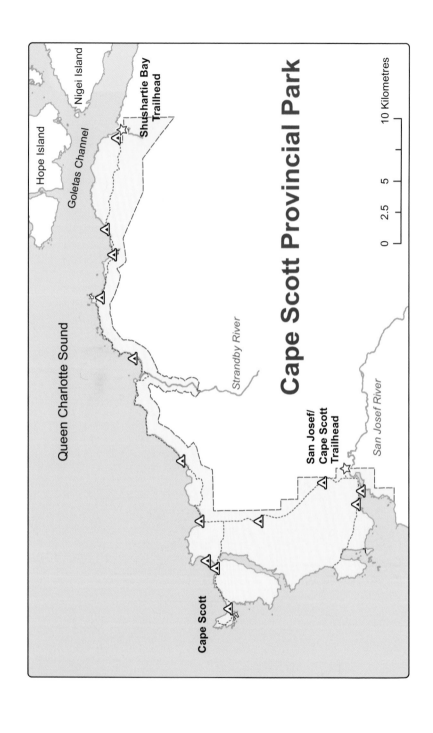

Cape Scott Provincial Park

Hope Island

Nigei Island

Shushartie Bay Trailhead

Goletas Channel

Queen Charlotte Sound

Strandby River

San Josef/ Cape Scott Trailhead

San Josef River

Cape Scott

0   2.5   5   10 Kilometres

CAPE SCOTT
and the
NORTH COAST TRAIL

Hiking Vancouver Island's Wildest Coast

MARIA I. BREMNER

Harbour Publishing

HARBOUR PUBLISHING CO. LTD.
PO Box 219, Madeira Park, BC, V0N 2H0
www.harbourpublishing.com

Edited by Hazel Boydell
Indexed by Brianna Cerkiewicz
Text design by Shed Simas and Mary White
Cover design by Brianna Cerkiewicz
Maps by David J. Turner
All photos by Maria I. Bremner except where otherwise noted
Title page photo: Chris Darimont, raincoast.org
Printed and bound in Canada

Excerpt from "Rain and the Rhinoceros" (page v) by Thomas Merton, from *Raids on the Unspeakable*, copyright © 1966 by The Abbey of Gethsemani, Inc. Reprinted by permission of New Directions Publishing Corp.

Canada Council   Conseil des arts
for the Arts   du Canada

BRITISH COLUMBIA
ARTS COUNCIL
An agency of the Province of British Columbia

Harbour Publishing acknowledges the support of the Canada Council for the Arts, which last year invested $157 million to bring the arts to Canadians throughout the country. We also gratefully acknowledge financial support from the Government of Canada through the Canada Book Fund and from the Province of British Columbia through the BC Arts Council and the Book Publishing Tax Credit.

Cataloguing data available from Library and Archives Canada
ISBN 978-1-55017-691-9 (paper)
ISBN 978-1-55017-692-6 (ebook)

To the big hearts and lone wolves of the world
for making this a unique and beautiful place.

The rain surrounded the cabin ... with a whole world of meaning,
of secrecy, of rumor. Think of it: all that speech pouring down,
selling nothing, judging nobody, drenching the thick mulch of
dead leaves, soaking the trees, filling the gullies and crannies of
the wood with water, washing out the places where men have
stripped the hillside ... Nobody started it, nobody is going to
stop it. It will talk as long as it wants, the rain. As long as it talks I
am going to listen.

—THOMAS MERTON
from "Rain and the Rhinoceros"

CONTENTS

Starfish sunset, Nels Bight. *Photo: Steve Fines*

THE BEACH

On the beach, your heart is
pounding, pounding.
It's just the rush of the waves—
like memories, half-formed questions
endless and gone.

Under the light, a tiny figure fades away:
overtaken by a place,
overturned like a simple pebble
caught in the chaos of a methodical tide.

You step on to the beach,
no such religion at hand,
with everything in your heart,
you see
the world.

—MARIA I. BREMNER

INTRODUCTION

CAPE SCOTT PROVINCIAL PARK lies as far north as you can travel on Vancouver Island before plunging into the unforgiving Pacific Ocean. In the late fall and winter, the beaches are empty. The hiking season has ended and cable cars are susceptible to being washed out by record-level rains and wind. For the long wet season, the wild things roam this land without intrusion.

On clear summer nights, bears busy themselves doing what bears do—snuffling through thick mats of seaweed in search of oceanic delicacies. Fat sand fleas hurl themselves into the air to avoid bear-sized mouths. Wolves course the beaches unseen but for their morning tracks. The crowded darkness of the forest keeps permanent company with the sound of pounding surf.

The North Island is a rugged, harsh and stunningly beautiful landscape. It is a stranger who keeps her secrets tight, and a friend who always offers unexpected gifts.

Cape Scott is a wilderness park with deep human histories. This guidebook tells you what to expect on the trails, where to find the sandy beaches, and what plants and animals you may encounter. This information will not only help you prepare for the area's isolation and ruggedness, and better navigate the

Barnacle Beach. *Photo: Steve Fines*

trails, but also to appreciate the rich natural and human history of the region.

The rest of what Cape Scott has to offer—the magic at the heart of this place—is up to you to find. And there is no travel itinerary for that.

ABOUT CAPE SCOTT AND THE NORTH COAST TRAIL

CAPE SCOTT PROVINCIAL PARK is remote, wild, and coastal. Enveloping the northernmost tip of Vancouver Island, this protected area represents some of the most iconic coastal wilderness of the Pacific Northwest. The area has been known for the lighthouse on the cape since 1960 and for pristine sandy beaches for much longer. The park was created in 1973 with the later addition of the eastern Shushartie Bay section and the development of the North Coast Trail. Now totalling more than 22,300 ha (around 55,000 acres), the park includes 115 km (around 71 mi) of coastline with rocky headlands, pebbly shores, and long sandy beaches. Inland, rainforest, estuaries, rivers, and unique bogs protect rich and diverse habitats for a wide array of animal and plant species. For visitors willing to travel the distance, the simple act of experiencing this place provides no better reward.

REGIONAL LOCATION

LOCATED ON THE NORTHERN tip of Vancouver Island, Cape Scott Provincial Park is about a 7.5-hour drive from Victoria (around 563 km or 350 mi). There are two trailheads: the San Josef/

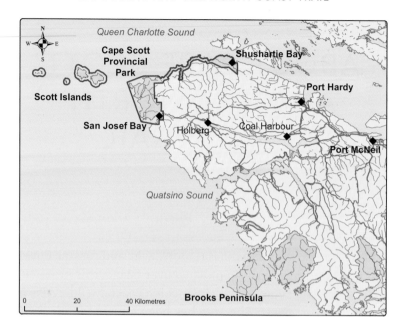

Cape Scott trailhead, in a parking lot 64 km (around 40 mi) west of Port Hardy and accessible by highways and private, active logging roads; and a second at Shushartie Bay, accessible by water taxi.

WHAT TO EXPECT

AS FAR AWAY FROM the urban capital of Victoria as Vancouver Island allows, Cape Scott's isolation and remoteness has sheltered the area from human development and population growth. In the absence of big-box development and busy intersections, wildlife flourishes. Despite the telltale pockmarks of logging visible by satellite, the park contains vast natural spaces and rugged coastal wilderness that is utterly spectacular. On arrival in Port Hardy—the official launch pad for the North Coast Trail—the line separating human habitation and the wild blurs.

FAST FACTS: CAPE SCOTT PROVINCIAL PARK

Size	22,300 ha (around 55,000 acres)
Location	Northwestern tip of Vancouver Island, BC
Nearest town	Holberg (population approximately 200)
Length of hiking trails	80.4 km (around 50 mi) of unique trails. Within this, the North Coast Trail comprises 43.1 km (26.8 mi)
Number of beach campsites	Ten: San Josef Bay first and second beaches, Lowrie Bay, Experiment Bight, Guise Bay, Nels Bight, Nissen Bight, Wolftrack Beach, Shuttleworth Bight, and Cape Sutil
Most popular campsite	Nels Bight
Length of coastline	115 km (around 71 mi); 30 km (around 18 mi) of beaches
Designation as a Provincial Park	1973
Completion of the North Coast Trail extension	2008
Dominant ecosystem	Coastal Western Hemlock Biogeoclimatic Zone

Steps from downtown, you'll see healthy populations of eagles, salmon, birds, and seals. Once on the trail, you truly enter their world. The diversity of wildlife—migratory seabirds, salmon, amphibians, sea lions, wolves, elk, and bears to name a few—provides testament to the richness of this coastal ecosystem.

However wild, Cape Scott is not untouched. A rich and diverse human history echoes in the wind. The Kwakwa̱ka'wakw First Nations have inhabited the Cape Scott region for millennia. Their legends and lore weave through the region, and a cultural and spiritual tie to this land is maintained today. Abundant natural resources traditionally supported the Kwakwa̱ka'wakw way of life and dictated not just seasonal patterns

3

of resource gathering but also complex social structures. The North Island later attracted European explorers and traders seeking wealth from these natural resources. Whether it was a thirst for lumber, coal, furs, or fish, the North Island was the epicentre of a resource economy for much of the 19th and 20th centuries. Exploration and trade paved the way for settlers who arrived in the region with dreams to eke out a living off the land. Moss-covered remnants of the Cape Scott settlement can still be seen today. The history section of this book (page 140) provides greater detail.

In addition to the human history and culture, the beaches of Cape Scott also serve as a sobering reminder of our global connectedness. As you hike along the coast and take in its stunning beauty, your attention can't help but shift to the plastic flotsam found on nearly every beach. Much of it is debris from the devastating 2011 tsunami in Japan, although there was already a significant amount of plastic washed up prior to this tragedy. Even in this remote part of the world, seemingly far away from civilization, it is clear that no environment is free from the impact of our disposable society.

TOPOGRAPHY, TERRAIN AND HIKING CONDITIONS

THE SPECTRUM OF HIKING opportunities in Cape Scott is suitable for any ability. Whether you want to take the family for an easy stroll to San Josef Bay or traverse the entire length of the park, Cape Scott provides something for all nature lovers. The completion of the North Coast Trail in 2008 allows a hike from trailhead to trailhead for a distance of at least 58 km (around 36 mi). When you add in optional daytrips to explore the park's west beaches—the Cape Scott lighthouse, San Josef Bay, Mount St. Patrick, and Lowrie Bay—it is possible to log over 100 km (around 62 mi).

Rugged coastal terrain characterizes Cape Scott Provincial Park. With 115 km (around 71 mi) of dramatic weather-worn coastline, Cape Scott offers almost every kind of beach imaginable—long stretches of sand, pebbles, cobblestones, rocky headlands, and protected coves. Some beaches provide gentle, sandy havens. Others offer unforgiving terrain. Steep, off-cambered slopes, slippery boulders, foot-abusing cobblestones, tangles of driftwood, and enormous beds of soft seaweed all combine to create definite challenges. Tired hikers can find these beach conditions difficult, especially at the end of a long day. Knee and ankle injuries are the most common ailments. In addition, the exposed beach can subject you to every kind of weather—warm sun, howling wind, or driving rain. Consider the time of year you intend to hike and be prepared for all possibilities.

Away from the beaches, the forest surrounds you. A dense network of towering conifers, ferns, salal, beds of moss, and varied underbrush creates a true rainforest that often drips from rainfall, wet wind, or ocean mist. While most of the trails in the park lie close to sea level, expect some elevation change as you head inland. Several beach access points have very steep and slippery slopes. Harsh weather exacerbates the effort, turning every climb into a scramble. In some areas ropes or steps provide assistance.

Mount St. Patrick marks the highest point in the park at 420 m (around 1,378 ft). However, unless you choose to specifically add this to your trip, there is no need to hike to the summit of this challenging mountain. Along the North Coast Trail, the highest elevation is 225 m (around 738 ft) at the top of the upland bog near Shushartie Bay. Gaining this elevation with a full pack can be a challenge. Even when not climbing, hikers encounter rough sections in the forest—storm-fallen branches, old stumps, and roots lie in wait to trip tired travellers. Add mud to this equation and it can make for a tiring slog.

Located in the rainiest zone in British Columbia, the terrain of Cape Scott is shaped from water and moisture. Creeks and river systems weave throughout the landscape and join the ocean. Several estuaries—ecosystems where salt water and fresh water mix—exist at the mouths of the San Josef, Strandby, Nahwitti, and Shushartie Rivers, creating rich habitats that attract a proliferation of waterfowl. The Hansen Lagoon, a 5-km (around 3-mi) long saltwater marsh and mud flats, is an important stopover for migratory waterfowl. There are many water sources along the trail (the best ones are noted in the maps and trail descriptions), but it is important to recognize that aside from major creeks and rivers, many of these water sources are seasonal. If you are hiking at the end of a long, dry summer, anticipate drier conditions.

A signature of the park is its upland bog ecosystems. Located throughout the park, but particularly prevalent on the higher plateaus, these bogs are sensitive and unique ecosystems that provide habitat for amphibians and plants. The bogs resemble a muskeg-like landscape with exposed, stunted vegetation, spongy ground, trickling rivulets, and stagnant pools. Boardwalks protect the sensitive bogs (and your feet) in the wettest areas, but the terrain and climate make for some very muddy hiking.

Other striking features of the Cape Scott area include rocky caves, cliffs, and sea stacks (rock formations eroded into pillars

Looking west from the tombolo, about 3 km west of Cape Sutil.

by the sea). San Josef Bay provides a great opportunity to explore these, especially when at low tide. Sand dunes and beach meadows also make Guise Bay a worthwhile trip.

CLIMATE

CAPE SCOTT PROVINCIAL PARK has a temperate marine climate and receives a significant amount of rain. An average of 2,650 mm (around 104 in) of rain soaks the region every year. The town of Holberg, just 30 km southwest from Cape Scott, ranks number two on Canada's list of highest average yearly rainfall with 3,819 mm (150 in). Even in prime hiking season, from June to the end of September, it rains an average of 17 days every month. The Pacific Coast is by far the rainiest region in Canada and within this region, the North Island is home to a leader. In

CLIMATE DATA FOR CAPE SCOTT WEATHER STATION

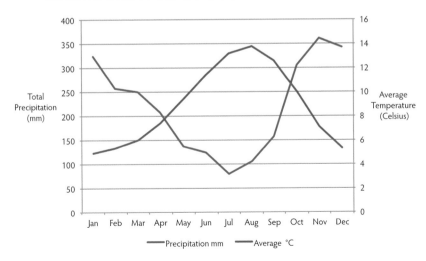

Source: *Environment Canada 2014, "Canadian Climate Normals 1971–2000"*

Canada, only five weather stations receive more annual precipitation and Cape Scott ranks in the 97th percentile of wet places worldwide! Winter temperatures rarely allow for snowfall, but year-round conditions are wet, wild, and windy. Frequent storms bring rapid flooding and winds that can reach speeds over 100 km (around 62 mi) per hour.

In summer, conditions are more hospitable for outdoor enthusiasts. Rainfall is considerably less and the sun shines. However, don't expect to be basking in a bikini—winds continue to blow in the summer months, pushing moisture-laden air over the land and keeping the temperature cool. The June to September daily average is only 13° C. Harsh weather can roll in quickly, bringing strong winds and rainfall. Plan for cool conditions and rain. If you get a clear window of weather during your trip, it will be that much more of a treat. Remember, you are in a unique rainforest ecosystem that depends on these wet conditions.

A COMPARISON OF THE NORTH COAST AND WEST COAST TRAILS

COMPLETED IN 2008, THE North Coast Trail draws more people every year. Between 2012 and 2013, the number of campers at Cape Scott increased almost 30 percent as the North Coast Trail became more known. However, it remains a far cry from the near-celebrity status of the West Coast Trail and has been billed by some as the "undiscovered West Coast Trail." But does it really have all the beauty without the crowds, the same wilderness exhilaration without waitlists, the bliss without the blisters? For the droves of West Coast Trail veterans who want to try something equally epic and beautiful without the crowds, here is a quick overview of how the two trails compare.

THE NORTH COAST AND WEST COAST TRAILS

	NORTH COAST TRAIL	WEST COAST TRAIL
Operations and Designation	Provincially operated by BC Parks and the Park Facility Operator. NCT is located within Cape Scott Provincial Park.	Federally operated by Parks Canada. One of three units within Pacific Rim National Park Reserve.
Hiking Distance	58–78 km (around 36–49 mi). Shorter if hiking from trailhead to trailhead, longer if including Nels Bight and the lighthouse.	75 km (around 45 mi)
Time	5–8 days. Dependent on the inclusion of Cape Scott and the lighthouse.	5–7 days
Estimated Total Cost per Person (not including fuel or parking)	$235. Backcountry camping fee: $10 per night (assumes seven nights); water taxi: $90; shuttle service: $75.	$279. Reservation fee: $24.50; backcountry camping fee and permit: $127.50; ferry fees for Gordon River and Nitinat Narrows: $16 each; bus fare one-way from Port Renfrew to Bamfield: $95.
Reservations	Not necessary for the park but required for the water taxi and shuttle service.	Recommended. A handful of standby spaces are provided daily.
Human Use	5,700 campers in 2012/13. Note that this includes people who only camped in the west side of the park. Expect to see very few people while hiking the North Coast Trail.	Over 5,700 in 2013. Sixty-eight hikers are permitted to start each day. Expect crowded food lockers and campsites.
Climate	Marine temperate: • annual average rainfall: 2,650 mm (104 in) • average temperature June to September: 12.8° C (55° F). High winds (above 100 km or 62 mi per hour) are possible through the summer.	Marine temperate: • annual average rainfall: 2,890 mm (114 in) • average temperature June to September: 13.9° C (57° F) Heavy morning fog is common, especially in July and August.

THE NORTH COAST AND WEST COAST TRAILS (CONT.)

	NORTH COAST TRAIL	WEST COAST TRAIL
Hiking Terrain	Roughly half forest and half beach hiking. The beach walking can be very difficult and tedious. Forest trails are rough and muddy. Lots of boardwalks (extremely slippery when wet) and two cable cars.	Primarily along the beach and rocky coastal shelf. Forest terrain is steep and rough. There are many ladders and water crossings (both bridges and cable cars).
Scenery	8/10 (spectacular but, overall, not as pretty as on the WCT)	9/10 (world renowned)
Wildlife Viewing	Yes. Bear, eagle, and wolf sightings are more common.	Yes, but not as frequent as the NCT given a higher volume of people. Whale and bear sightings are common.
Trailhead Location	Northwest coast of Vancouver Island.	Southwest coast of Vancouver Island.
Transportation from Victoria	7.5 hours by car (around 563 km or 350 mi). Shuttle and bus services available.	2–4 hours by car (around 100–200 km or 62–124 mi), dependent on whether you choose the southern Gordon River or northern Pachena Bay trailhead. Shuttle and bus services available.
Culture and History	Within the traditional territory of the Kwakwa̱ka̱'wakw. The area was a busy hub of the fur trade and commerce in the mid-1800s. Sites and artifacts of two major settlement attempts by pioneers and a World War II radar station.	Passes through the traditional territory of the Pacheedaht, Ditidaht and the Huu-ay-aht people (Nuu-cha-nulth, formerly known as Nootka, peoples). The hiking route was once a telegraph line and lifesaving route for shipwrecked mariners.

The North Coast Trail lacks the tent cities and bulging food lockers of the West Coast Trail and has more visible wildlife and less garbage. You don't get a certificate for finishing the North Coast Trail, and there certainly aren't any places to grab a burger, beer, or freshly boiled crab on the trail. Due to its remoteness, the North Coast Trail will likely always be the quieter, rougher, and less popular of the two.

WHO SHOULD HIKE IT?

WHILE THE WIDE RANGE of hiking options is enough to fill the hearts of nature lovers, adventurists, solitude-seekers, and all those in between, the North Coast Trail is not for everyone. The marine climate and remoteness should be a significant consideration in your decision whether to tackle this trail. It should also be central in your preparations. People who underestimate the hazards of a wet climate can quickly find themselves in the dangerous throes of hypothermia, even in the summer.

While not extreme, the terrain is strenuous, requiring a reasonable degree of fitness and outdoor experience (working out in the gym is no substitute). That said, a person in good hiking fitness and properly prepared with the right food, gear, and attitude can hike Cape Scott and the North Coast Trail. Because of its remoteness, terrain, and climate you should also have some prior experience with backpacking. A relaxing weekend trip to Nels Bight or San Josef Bay would be a great way of getting accustomed to the region.

The North Coast Trail is not recommended for people with knee injuries due to the slippery and steep inclines and declines. Nor is it recommended for children under 12 unless they are accustomed to hiking long days in the wilderness and preparations can be made to allow them to hike without substantial weight.

PLANNING YOUR TRIP

TRIP PLANNING AND PREPARATIONS (or lack thereof) can make or break your trip.

WHEN TO HIKE

WHILE CAPE SCOTT PROVINCIAL Park is open year-round, the best season to visit is summer, particularly July and August when there is the least rainfall and the temperatures are warmest. Even so, any true West Coaster will remind you to always be prepared for, and expect, rain, wind, and cooler temperatures in this region. In the summer, the trails are drier (but not dry) and easier (yet not easy). In this season, camp chores go more smoothly and the reward of finishing a hard day beneath a starry sky is impossible to beat. The shoulder months of June and September are also excellent—there are fewer people and the weather conditions are still generally favourable.

There is a ranger yurt located at Cape Sutil that is staffed with Park Facility Operators from June 15 to Labour Day weekend (the first Monday in September). In the off-season (October to the end of April), fees are not collected and there is no regular maintenance of the park. However, if weather permits, day-hikes and overnighters can be enjoyed throughout the year.

Longer backpacking trips are not recommended in the off-season. Heavy, seemingly endless rainfall creates extremely muddy trail conditions and dangerously high river flow. Cable cars are usually dismantled in the off-season and fording the rivers is near impossible and certainly life-threatening. In addition, hurricane-force winds ravage the North Island during the winter months, leading to fallen trees and frigid conditions.

GETTING TO THE NORTH ISLAND

THERE ARE A NUMBER of ways to get to the North Island. With the exception of air travel, you should anticipate a full day to travel from Victoria or Vancouver to Port Hardy, your

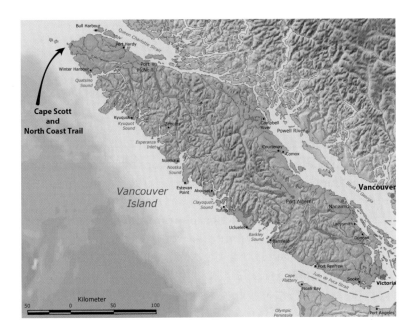

penultimate destination. Home to around 4,000 people, Port Hardy is the northern terminus of Highway 19 and the primary launch pad to Cape Scott. The North Coast Trail shuttle service operates from the marina in town. Port Hardy also offers the last chance of grocery and hardware stores to supply any forgotten items before you leave civilization. See Appendix 2: Service Providers and Other Useful Contacts for more information on travel providers.

TRANSIT TO PORT HARDY

FROM	VICTORIA	NANAIMO	CAMPBELL R.	VANCOUVER*
Distance	498 km 309 mi	387 km 240 mi	233 km 145 mi	477 km 296 mi
Car	6 hr	4 hr 40 min	3 hr	7 hr 30 min
Greyhound bus	9 hr 30 min	6 hr 30 min	3 hr 20 min	13 hr (not incl. transfer time in Nanaimo)

*NOTE: this route includes ferry travel but does not include wait time at ferry

- BY CAR: Driving to Port Hardy is relatively straightforward. From Victoria, take the Trans-Canada Highway (Hwy 1) heading north. At Nanaimo, the highway merges into Highway 19, continuing north to Parksville/Campbell River. Highway 19 continues all the way to Port Hardy. The stretch of Highway 19 that extends from Campbell River to Port Hardy has been named the North Island Route. Many sections of this route have been recently repaved; it is well maintained and double-lane much of the way. Once you leave Campbell River, the road becomes lonely—you're now heading into the North Island. As you crest the highway around Sayward, mist or rain can close around your vehicle and conifers watch as silent sentries. Keep an eye out for wildlife.

- BY PLANE: Pacific Coastal Airlines operate daily scheduled flights between the Port Hardy Airport (YZT) and Vancouver Airport's South Terminal (YVR). Flights take around an hour.

- BY FERRY: If you are coming from the mainland, take the ferry from North Vancouver's Horseshoe Bay to Departure Bay in Nanaimo. Alternatively, you can take the ferry from Tsawwassen to Swartz Bay, near Victoria, but it will mean more driving.

- BY BUS: Both Greyhound and IslandLinkBus offer daily service to Port Hardy from other Vancouver Island towns. On Greyhound, the trip from Nanaimo to Port Hardy will typically take 6.5 hours. The Victoria to Port Hardy route is approximately 9.5 hours. IslandLinkBus provides service between most Vancouver Island points and BC Ferries services at Nanaimo's Departure Bay. In the summer (May 19 to September 29), service is provided to Port Hardy every other day.

   BC Transit provides local transit service in the North Island region, including Port Hardy and Port McNeill.

TRAVEL TIPS

- TAKE BREAKS BUT DON'T DAWDLE. From Victoria to Port Hardy, you'll be logging just shy of 500 km (around 310 mi). See Regional Information (page 192) for some suggested rest areas along Highway 19 to stretch your legs, eat something, and use the bathroom.

- STOCK UP BEFORE YOU GET THERE! If you forget anything, Campbell River is the last town and major stop for supplies and fuel (there is an Esso gas station on the highway at Hyde Creek). When you arrive in Port Hardy, stores may be closed and shuttles leave too early to allow for last-minute stocking up on provisions.

- DRIVE SAFELY. Highway 19 is quiet, so be attentive for wildlife and other vehicles. Forestry is active on this side of the island so watch ahead for any slow-moving loads joining the highway. Highway 19 is well maintained but road conditions can be dangerous when heavy fog or rain sets in.

- BE PREPARED FOR LOGGING ROADS. The route to Cape Scott from Port Hardy requires more than 60 km (around 37 mi) of travel along gravel roads. You will likely encounter logging trucks. They are big, travel fast, and are often heavily loaded—meaning their braking time is much extended. Keep your headlights on at all times and drive attentively. Remember that on private roads, logging trucks have right-of-way. Yield to them by pulling as far to the shoulder as possible without getting yourself stuck.

- CARRY A SPARE TIRE IN CASE OF A FLAT.

ACCOMMODATION

FINDING ACCOMMODATION ON THE North Island is easy and there is a spectrum of choice ranging from camping and hostels to high-end hotels and cabins.

In Port Hardy, hostels provide the most economical option. The North Coast Trail Backpacker's Hostel and C&N Backpackers Hostel both offer rooms for under $30 per night. A number of hotels and motels in Port Hardy are also within walking distance of cafes and the marina. For ultimate convenience, the Quarter Deck Inn is located right at the marina where the water taxi and shuttle leave.

For those wanting to sleep as close to the trailhead as possible, there are two campgrounds less than a kilometre from the San Josef/Cape Scott trailhead: the San Josef Heritage Park and the Western Forest Products private campgrounds. Just south of

Port Hardy is the Quatse River Regional Park and Campground, a very nice spot from which revenue benefits salmon enhancement activities. There are two recreation sites near the exit from Port Hardy to Holberg: Georgie Lake and Nahwitti Lake.

GETTING TO THE TRAILHEADS

GETTING TO EITHER OF the trailheads is straightforward. First decide which trailhead you will be starting from. If starting from the Shushartie Bay trailhead (east end of the trail), you will be arriving by water taxi from Port Hardy. If the San Josef/ Cape Scott trailhead (the west end) is your launch pad, then the logging road toward Holberg from Port Hardy will be your portal in. Hiking the trail from east to west is best for both transportation logistics and scenery (see "Which way to hike it" (page 11) for more commentary on this).

The second major consideration is whether you will use your own vehicle to get to the trailhead. If you are hiking the North Coast Trail end-to-end, take the shuttle at one end, and the water taxi at the other. It is the most relaxed, efficient, and safe option. You don't have to deal with the complicated and potentially expensive retrieval of your car after you have returned to Port Hardy. You can leave the dangerous and rugged logging road driving to someone who is experienced with the route. Also, you avoid risking flat tires or vehicle theft. Considering

For some people it's a race. For others, it's an escape …
—GEORGE BURROUGHS,
North Coast Trail Shuttle driver,
on what motivates hikers

the travel time, the shuttle is a bargain and if you arrange travel with other passengers can be very affordable.

The North Coast Trail Shuttle (see page 212 for details) advertises itself as "your one-stop land and water taxi transportation." It runs from May 15 to September 15. You can pay the $10 per night backcountry fee at the shuttle office prior to the departure or book online and show proof of payment. In addition, the shuttle sells trail maps and rents marine VHF radios.

SHUSHARTIE BAY TRAILHEAD

The Shushartie Bay trailhead is reached by water taxi. Operated by the North Coast Trail Shuttle, the *Sea Legend 1,* is a 32-foot, 12-passenger vessel. The cab of the water taxi is heated, and the ride is full of wildlife-watching opportunities, coastal beauty, and recitations of local lore. Keep your eyes out for porpoises, humpback whales, eagles, and even the odd swimming wolf! The owner/operator, George, has fantastic stories to share.

See page 212 for water taxi details.

SAN JOSEF/CAPE SCOTT TRAILHEAD

The North Coast Trail Shuttle provides service to and from Port Hardy to the San Josef/Cape Scott trailhead. Personal vehicle parking is available for a small fee at the district lot located next to the company office/dock at the Quarterdeck Marina. See page 212 for more shuttle details.

Taking your own vehicle to the trailhead makes sense if you are just hiking the west side of the park (Cape Scott and the San Josef Bay areas) as an out-and-back. You should have good tires, keep your lights on, and be prepared to yield to logging trucks. Also, have a full tank of fuel, as the gas station at Holberg may be closed or out of fuel (fill up in Port McNeill if you are heading directly to the trailhead without visiting Port Hardy). Also note that BCAA does not cover towing from Cape Scott (if needed, this can cost over $500).

It is about 67 km (about 42 mi) from Port Hardy to the San Josef/Cape Scott trailhead. When the road is freshly graded and visibility is good, it is realistic to travel about 50 km per hour. To get there:

- Take the marked turn-off to Holberg about 2 km (just over a mile) south of Port Hardy. There are signs to guide you the rest of the way.
- Travel west on a combination of public and privately owned forestry roads. These are mostly gravel. Again, be prepared for defensive action on the private logging roads—remember that trucks have right-of-way. You will pass two lakes (Kains Lake followed by Nahwitti Lake), a couple forest recreation sites, and the famous shoe tree—an old cedar snag covered with hundreds of shoes left by passing travellers. Apparently, it was started after a woman destroyed her shoes on the Cape Scott hike, and decided to make a tribute by nailing her shoes to the tree.
- Eventually, Holberg Road turns into NE 60 Road. Stay on this until you come to the small village of Holberg, located 46 km (around 29 mi) from the turn-off. The Scarlet Ibis pub, overlooking the quiet Holberg Inlet, is a good spot for hungry hikers looking for a bite to eat.
- From Holberg, continue on San Josef Main following the Cape Scott Provincial Park signs for an additional 19 km (around 12 mi).

At the trailhead, a large parking lot greets you—perhaps a surprise considering the remote location. You will find two wheelchair-accessible outhouses, a large shelter with picnic tables, an interpretive sign and information board, a hut for the park facility operator and ample parking room for vehicles and several large buses. In the mid-2000s, the provincial government considered putting a large, privately owned tourist accommodation here, alongside several other provincial parks.

The controversial strategy was shelved after much opposition to development within park boundaries.

Note that the parking lot is regularly visited by bears and that vehicles have been broken into. Do not leave bags unattended, keep vehicle windows closed, and take all valuables with you.

WILDERNESS AND CAMPING PERMITS

BACKCOUNTRY CAMPING FEES ARE collected in Cape Scott Provincial Park from May 1 to September 30. Fees are $10 per person, per night and $5 for children six to 15 years old. Fees go directly to trail and park maintenance. You can pay your fees in three ways:

· Self-registration envelopes provided at either of the two main trailheads. Be sure to bring cash in the exact amount you will need for your stay and deposit the envelope provided into the red vault.

· Online payment through the BC Parks Backcountry Registration System. This convenient system can be accessed from the BC Parks Cape Scott Provincial Park website (see Appendix 2, page 211).

· If you are travelling by the North Coast Trail shuttle or water taxi, you can pay at their office prior to departing or show proof of online payment.

Be sure to carry your receipt with you on your hike. You may be asked to provide it by Park Facility Operators patrolling the park and camping areas.

WHICH DIRECTION TO HIKE?

YOU CAN HIKE THE North Coast Trail from west to east (Cape Scott to Shushartie Bay) or the opposite. I have enjoyed each direction but recommend east to west for the following reasons:

- SAVE THE BEST FOR LAST. While the whole trail is wonderful, the most spectacular beaches are located at the west end. Here, there are also opportunities for day hikes, including to the lighthouse and Cape Scott area. By hiking from east to west, you will be better able to budget how much time you have at the end to enjoy these beaches.

- LOGISTICAL SECURITY. If anything were to go wrong on your trip (whether injury or other unforeseen event), hiking from east to west allows you to skip the Cape Scott section and head directly to the San Josef/Cape Scott trailhead. In contrast, if you are hiking from west to east, you will have to have a very good sense of how long the hike will take you to avoid missing the morning water taxi from Shushartie Bay. In addition, while the Shushartie Bay camp is cozy, it is void of an immediate water source. Finally, if you miss your shuttle from the San Josef/Cape Scott trailhead, you can at least try to get a ride with a nice stranger from the parking lot. Shushartie Bay's isolation allows no such backup plan.

- EXIT TIME. The shuttle van picks up at the San Josef/Cape Scott trailhead parking lot in the early afternoon. You can camp at Eric Lake or San Josef Bay the night before and easily make it to the parking lot in time. After a night at San Josef Bay, it's a luxuriously slow morning dawdle along the easy 2 km (about a mile) trail for your designated pick-up time.

For more details on suggested itineraries see page 216.

WHAT TO PACK

THE CONSTANT STRUGGLE FOR backpackers is the compromise of what to carry. Too much and you risk injury or grumpiness, too little and you may struggle to keep your belly full or stay dry and warm. The ultra-light zealots of the world are up the night before shaving off toothbrush handles, excess body hair, and pulling out the internal frames from their packs. Others stumble under loads including bottles of booze, coolers, and full-size shampoo and conditioner bottles.

As a general rule, your pack should weigh about 30 percent of your body weight. This allows little room for luxuries. Consider the following recommended equipment list for Cape Scott and the North Coast Trail and tailor according to your personal needs, preference, and peril!

Choose lightweight gear wherever possible. Avoid cotton and down, which gets heavy when wet. Opt for waterproof and/or breathable clothing that is loose fitting and made of quick-dry materials, synthetic or Merino wool. Keep everything that you want dry (e.g. clothes, sleeping bag, books, matches, etc.) in Ziploc or dry bags.

Steller's jay looks to share a snack. *Photo: Graham Smith*

SAMPLE EQUIPMENT LIST

HIKING

- ☐ Hiking boots[1]
- ☐ Backpack (with rain cover)
- ☐ Gaiters
- ☐ Water purification equipment (tablets, filter, UV pen, or drops)
- ☐ Water bottles (two one-litre)
- ☐ Ziploc or waterproof bags (for food waste and anything that you want to keep dry)
- ☐ Wide-brimmed hat
- ☐ Sunglasses
- ☐ Sunblock
- ☐ Tide tables
- ☐ Maps
- ☐ Bear spray and/or bear bangers

CAMP AND COOKING

- ☐ Stove and fuel
- ☐ Cooking tools: pots, utensils, mugs, and a sharp knife
- ☐ Lighter, matches, and candles
- ☐ Ziploc to seal food and food waste
- ☐ Headlamp or flashlight with extra batteries
- ☐ Tent with waterproof fly
- ☐ Sleeping bag
- ☐ Sleeping pad
- ☐ Food. Choose high-energy, lightweight, low-smell items. Consider extra food to fuel the physical activity and in case of emergency.
- ☐ Food cache rope: 22 m (around 72 ft) of quarter-inch rope and two carabiners.
- ☐ Tarp and rope to string it up.

---

1 With ankle support, a waterproof/resistant outer and flexible rubber soles (for better traction than hard Vibram on slippery boardwalks, wet roots, and rocks).

PERSONAL
☐ Toilet paper
☐ Toiletries (avoid scented products)
☐ Medication as required

EMERGENCY
☐ Fire-starter sticks
☐ First-aid kit (including moleskin, tensor bandages, and antihistamine)
☐ Heavy-duty garbage bag[2]
☐ Sharp knife or multi-tool
☐ Pen and paper
☐ Compass
☐ Repair kit[3]

CLOTHES
☐ Waterproof jacket and pants
☐ Fleece jacket
☐ Lightweight wool or fleece sweater
☐ Long-sleeve base layer
☐ T-shirts (as needed)
☐ Toque
☐ Gloves
☐ Long underwear (top and bottom)
☐ Hiking pants
☐ Shorts
☐ Socks (around five pairs)
☐ Underwear

---

2 As an emergency tarp or to insulate a victim of hypothermia.
3 Heavy-duty needles, stove repair parts and tools, 9 m (around 30 ft) of fishing line, five safety pins, 5 m (around 16 ft) of duct tape, and a spare pack buckle.

MISCELLANEOUS/OPTIONAL

- ☐ Lightweight shoes or sandals for at camp
- ☐ Hiking staff or collapsible ski poles
- ☐ Bandanas
- ☐ Insect repellent
- ☐ Camera
- ☐ GPS
- ☐ Unscented wipes
- ☐ Satellite phone or marine VHF radio
- ☐ Guidebooks
- ☐ Collapsible water container (4 to 6 litres)

GETTING PREPARED:
TOP 10 THINGS TO DO BEFORE YOU GO

HIKING FOR DAYS THROUGH rough weather and challenging terrain with a heavy pack takes a good attitude and lots of stamina. The following are the top 10 things that will help you make the most of your backcountry vacation in Cape Scott.

1. GET IN SHAPE. A 72-year-old man with Parkinson's disease hiked the North Coast Trail, but that doesn't mean anyone can. Be honest with yourself about your physical abilities. If you are physically prepared, you will see and enjoy more, and be more resilient to whatever challenges come your way. Start training well in advance (not the weekend before), and be willing to cancel if you are injured, however slight (this terrain exacerbates knee, back, and ankle injuries).

2. GET EXPERIENCED. You must be prepared for 5 to 8 days of isolated backcountry travel that will include a temperate rainforest climate, uneven terrain, slippery boardwalks, and wildlife. As a relatively young and isolated trail, the North Coast Trail is

less-travelled and wilder than most backpacking trips. You need to be self-sufficient. Don't unwrap and try your new stove for the first time on the trail. Test your gear, know how to use it, learn to safely cache food independently if needed, and familiarize yourself with good backcountry etiquette before you leave.

3. BREAK IN YOUR BOOTS. Hiking footwear is perhaps the most important piece of equipment on this trip but, if it doesn't fit you right, every single step will be torture. To avoid blisters, break in new boots before you begin your hike. Also ensure that your feet are as dry as possible when hiking. Waterproof your hiking boots if they aren't already. When you are on the trail, do not wait for a blister to develop. At the first signs of any itchiness or soreness, stop and apply moleskin or duct tape.

4. FIND A FRIEND TO GO WITH. It is safer and smarter to have a partner on this trip. The most common injuries that occur in Cape Scott Park are ankle and knee strains. (Regardless of your fitness, this can happen.) Injury, poor weather, encounters with wildlife, and other unforeseen events are always better handled with good company.

5. RESERVE THE SHUTTLE AND WATER TAXI. Reserving your spot on the shuttle and water taxi in advance will increase the chance of travelling on your preferred dates, as well as saving a few bucks by coordinating with other travellers.

6. LEAVE A TRIP PLAN. See page 220 for a sample trip plan to leave with a friend or family member, including your planned route and anticipated return date. Should anything go wrong, this will give emergency services a much better chance of finding you.

7. TAKE TIDE TABLES AND KNOW HOW TO READ THEM. As rhythmic and beautiful as the tide may be, it can also cause logistical

problems as certain sections of the trail are impassable at high tide. Before you go, print the tide tables for the period of your hike (tides change from day to day, and from year to year). Fisheries and Oceans Canada provides times and heights for high and low tide. See page 213 for details.

8. TRAIL INFORMATION AND CONDITIONS. In the days and weeks leading up to your trip, be sure to check the BC Parks Cape Scott Provincial Park website for any alerts or advisories.

9. PACK FOR THE COAST. Prepare for wind, rain, and cold. Even if the forecast is a clear run of beautiful blue skies, be ready for poor conditions. Mist is normal and should be considered when deciding what to pack. Torrential rain and violent storms can occur at any time of year including the summer. Tarps, waterproof and breathable clothing, and warm soups are all things to consider. See the recommended equipment list (page 23) for more specific suggestions.

10. READ THE WILDLIFE SAFETY SECTION. Hiking in wild places requires that people respect the area and leave it as pristine as possible. Avoid encounters with wildlife for both human and animal welfare. Backcountry etiquette, particularly food storage, cleaning, and cooking should be taken seriously. Mishandling food will attract animals and have an impact on the habituation of bears and wolves to humans. In the unlikely event that you do have an encounter with wildlife, know how to respond to avoid conflict.

COASTAL CAMPING AND HIKING TIPS

HOW DO YOU CAMP in the rain? What considerations should you have about the ocean? Here are some tips specific to camping on the coast of the Pacific Northwest.

CONSIDER THE TIDE, rip currents, and rogue waves: Do not underestimate the power of the ocean. Strong winds or storms can elevate tides and create hazardous conditions. Be attentive to your surroundings when on the coast. As mentioned earlier, carry tide tables so that you can plan your hike accordingly (several points are passable only at lower tides). Keep a watchful eye for rogue waves whenever hiking along the coast. If you are tempted to go for a swim, be conservative. Powerful currents and unexpected large waves have killed many people who have been taken off-guard. Respect the ocean and keep a distance from the pounding surf when conditions seem uncertain. There are no lifeguards to perform rescues.

WEAR LAYERS. Regardless of the climate, backpacking is hard work. One moment, you will be working up a sweat as you huff up a hill, the next moment you could be shivering as a cold, misty wind blows in. The best way to deal with this is to dress in layers, and to have your waterproof shell close at hand in case of rain. Put your coat on at the first rain as there is a good chance you will not have time or resources to dry out damp clothes.

SET UP A TARP. Whether at camp or at a lunch stop, always look for ways to keep yourself and your gear dry. Unless clear skies are certain, tarp your camp area and use the natural shelter of forest cover. Weather on the coast can change quickly and shelter can make the difference between a comfortable night and a wet one.

BE AWARE OF HYPOTHERMIA. It most often occurs in mild weather (0° to 10° C or 32° to 50° F), can happen extremely quickly, and can kill. Cool temperatures, perspiration, wind, fatigue, and rain are all contributing factors. Prevention is the best measure, as well as recognizing and acting on early signs immediately.

Stay well-hydrated, even when the weather is cold and your urge to drink is not as strong.

Stay dry and wear layers of warm, windproof, and water-repellent clothing in chill, wet weather. Use synthetic, quick-wicking fabrics. Never use cotton. Pack a toque (or two) for emergencies—a significant amount of body heat is lost through your head. Always keep dry, spare clothing in your pack, and take care to keep your sleeping bag and matches dry.

Symptoms of hypothermia include chills and shivering, poor coordination, sluggish thinking, and slurred speech. This is followed by irrational thinking, incoherence, blue skin, and slowed pulse and respiration. When in danger of hypothermia, keep moving and make big decisions while your mind is clear. Monitor each other and be insistent with members of your hiking party if they show signs.

Caves at Tripod Beach. *Photo: Andrew Bruce Lau*

If a member of your team shows signs, replace their wet clothes with dry ones, insulate the victim from the ground, and provide warmth. You can do this by a pre-warmed sleeping bag (a warm water bottle in the bag is one way), providing skin contact with another body, building a fire, and feeding the victim carbohydrates and warm fluids.

BEACH CAMPING. Beach camping has unique factors to consider:
- The tide: Consult tide tables and set up your tent above the high tide line (if you aren't familiar with coastal environments, this can be surprisingly high). Look for the strandline—the farthest point of the high tide marked by a line of seaweed and ocean debris.
- Cleaning: Beaches are the ideal place to do camp dishes. Wash your dishes in the ocean whenever possible, and avoid the use of soap. Sand serves as a natural scrubber and washing in the ocean prevents the creeks from contamination from the cumulative residue of many campers. The ocean tides provide a constant influx of fresh water and ocean life to take away particles of food debris. You can even give yourself a sand-exfoliation treatment that would probably sell for hundreds of dollars at a city spa.
- Wildlife: Intertidal zones are a wildlife haven for sea birds, sea lions, and otters. They are also used as foraging and travel routes for bears, wolves, cougars, and deer. As such, you should exercise special caution and camp hygiene in these areas.

COMMUNICATIONS AND EVACUATIONS

THINK TWICE ABOUT RELYING on your cell phone for an emergency device. There is no cell reception in Cape Scott Provincial Park (in fact, cell phone reception starts to get patchy after Campbell River). Consider carrying a marine VHF radio, which you can rent from North Coast Trail Shuttle Ltd. In case of emergency, you can use this to call the company's office or the coast guard to arrange for an evacuation.

DOGS

AT THE TIME OF publication, dogs are not permitted in Cape Scott Provincial Park. Wolves have attacked many pet dogs in this park and off-leash dogs can provoke a bear attack. While you may want to share this amazing experience with your pet, respect the environment and leave Fluffy at home.

WILDLIFE SAFETY

REMEMBER THAT YOU ARE a guest in this environment. It is your responsibility to help prevent wild animals growing conditioned to humans and their food. Irresponsible behaviour can prove fatal—usually for the animals. Food-conditioned wildlife become accustomed to humans and can threaten park visitors as they roam in search of an easy meal. Conservation officers are then forced to destroy them when they become aggressive towards humans. Remember, a fed bear is a dead bear. If you encounter a bear, wolf, or cougar, report the sighting to a conservation officer. BC Parks provides clear advice on how to avoid encounters with wildlife. The following has been adapted from their website:

PARKING
Lock your vehicle and keep windows closed. Do not leave food or other attractants in your vehicle (if you must, secure them in your trunk). Bears have broken into vehicles parked in Cape Scott Provincial Park.

CAMPING AND FOOD

· The best way to avoid wildlife encounters is to prepare and store food properly. Animals are attracted by the smell of food, so reduce or eliminate odours by following this advice:

· Cook and eat meals away from your tent so food odours do not linger. Avoid spills while cooking; change out of and cache any clothes that you spill on before retiring. An ideal camp should have a sleeping area upwind of the cooking and food storage areas and all three should be at least 100 m (about 300 ft) apart.

· Avoid smelly foods, especially meat and fish. Bacon is said to be a particularly favourable scent to bears.

· Clean up immediately and thoroughly. Never leave cooking utensils, grease, or dishwater lying around. Wash either directly in the ocean, or in a container and dispose of grey water in the ocean.

· Food leftovers should be carried out with the garbage.

· Cache everything with an odour—your food, cookware, toothpaste, medication, insect repellent, other toiletries, garbage, and even water bottles if you use drink mixes in them. Bears have been noted to have a fondness for toothpaste. Use airtight containers if possible, and store them in one of the metal food lockers provided at every designated campsite.

· Know how to make your own food cache in case you find yourself camping outside of a designated campsite. A rope cache should be at least 12 metres off the ground and at least 5 metres from the tree trunk.

- If you are camping where there are no pit toilets, use areas below the high tide mark and away from camp, in an area of high tidal exchange for toilets. Do not use the upland areas, as human excrement will attract wildlife to trails and camps.

- Do not throw garbage in the pit toilets. If you pack it in, pack it out!

HIKING

- Make noise. Most animals would like to avoid you as much as you would like to avoid them. The best way to avoid an encounter while hiking is to make noise by whistling or talking, giving the animal notice that you're close by. Surprise encounters make an animal feel threatened and it may fight to defend itself.

- Travel with friends. Solo hikers are at a greater risk of wildlife attacks than groups so pair up with a friend or find other hikers.

- Stay clear of dead wildlife. Carcasses attract bears and other carnivores. Circling crows, ravens, or vultures are a sign of carrion, as is the smell of rotting meat. Avoid the area and leave immediately. Report the location of dead wildlife to park staff.

A proper campsite should be at least 100 metres away from food storage and cooking.

- Carry bear spray and know how to use it. Pepper sprays can be effective in preventing an encounter becoming an attack but should not be used as a substitute for preventative measures. If you test your bear spay, be sure to spray it in the direction of the wind to avoid it blowing right back into your face!

- Be mindful of children and pets. Do not allow children to wander and play away from camp. Keep them close to adults at all times. Do not bring pets into the park.

By taking these precautions, you should avoid direct contact with animals. But you should also be prepared for how to act if you do encounter a bear, cougar, or wolf.

BEARS
In this book, "bear" refers to black bears. There have been rare sightings of grizzly bears on Vancouver Island but their normal habitat is the mainland.

- Bears are amazing athletes—as fast as a racehorse, strong swimmers, and agile tree climbers. They have good eyesight, good hearing, and an acute sense of smell. They are omnivores—surprise encounters often happen when their noses are buried deep into a patch of salal bushes, or rooting for other food.

- Be especially cautious of moms with cubs to protect. They are more likely to be aggressive.

- If you spot a bear, make a wide detour and leave the area immediately. Watch for signs: tracks, droppings, overturned rocks, rotten trees torn apart, clawed, bitten, or rubbed trees, bear trails, fresh diggings, and trampled vegetation all suggest bears have been in the area.

- If you do encounter a bear and it does not move away, back off slowly. Speak in a low, calm voice and avoid making direct eye contact, which bears interpret as threatening. Do NOT flee.

- If the bear starts to follow, drop your pack or a piece of equipment in its path as a distraction. Only leave food as a last resort. A food-conditioned bear is a threat to the next human it meets.

- Aggressive behaviour includes jaw snapping, head lowering, ear flattening, woofing sounds, and growling. A bear may act defensively if it is surprised, or if it is protecting cubs, territory, or food. Wave your arms, talk in low tones and back away slowly. These actions will help identify you as not being a threat. Bears sometimes bluff their way out of a confrontation by charging and veering away at the last moment.

- Don't climb a tree—black bears can easily out-climb you.

- If the bear is exhibiting predatory behaviour, you should change your approach. Predatory behaviour includes following you, showing interest in you, and unprovoked attacks. Bears that enter a campsite or cooking area while you are there should be considered predatory. Jump up and down, wave your arms and yell. Try to look as large as possible. You are trying to demonstrate that you are not worth fighting. Have your bear spray at hand and be prepared to fight back.

- If you are actually attacked by a bear, do not play dead. Instead, fight back with all you have. Use anything at hand to protect yourself—pepper spray, rocks, sticks, and fists.

COUGARS

Cougars are secretive, solitary animals with astonishing predatory abilities. Fortunately, cougar sightings and human interactions are extremely rare. In the last century, only seven people have been killed by cougars in BC. If you do encounter a cougar, here are some tips:

· Stay calm and keep the cougar in view. Pick up any children—their noise and movements could provoke an attack.

· Back away slowly, and give the cougar a clear avenue of escape. Never run or turn your back on a cougar. Sudden movement may provoke an attack.

· Make yourself look as large and tall as possible (spread your arms and open your jacket).

· If a cougar shows interest or follows you, respond aggressively. Maintain eye contact, show your teeth, and make loud noise. Arm yourself with rocks or sticks as weapons. Crouch down as little as possible when bending down to pick these up from the ground.

· If a cougar attacks, fight back. Do not play dead. Convince the cougar you are a threat and not prey. Use anything you can as a weapon and focus your attack on the cougar's face and eyes.

WOLVES

British Columbia has two breeds of wolves—mainland timber wolves and their more relaxed coastal relatives. Coastal wolves have diets that can consist of up to 75 percent marine creatures—they dig for clams and eat barnacles. Wolves are usu-

Cougar. *Photo: David Akoubian*

ally secretive and will run away when they encounter people but, like bears, they can become habituated and may approach camping areas and hikers in search of food.

If a wolf appears and acts unafraid or aggressive, you should present yourself as a threat by taking the following action:

· Raise your arms and wave them in the air to make yourself appear larger.

· When in a group, act in unison to send a clear message to the wolves they are not welcome. Stand close together and synchronize noises to appear large and loud.

· Back away slowly. Do not turn your back on the wolf.

· Make noise and throw sticks, rocks, and sand at the wolf.

· If attacked, fight back with whatever you have.

Wolf at Shuttleworth Bight. *Photo: Graham Smith*

THE TRAIL

WITHIN THE FOLLOWING PAGES, a detailed description of each trail section is provided as follows:

TRAIL SECTION	MAP
1: Shushartie Bay to Skinner Creek, 0–8.7 km (0–5.4 mi)	Map 1
2: Skinner Creek to Nahwitti River and Cape Sutil, 8.7–16.6 km (5.4–10.3 mi)	Map 2
3: Cape Sutil to Irony Creek (Shuttleworth Bight), 16.6–23.8 km (10.3–14.8 mi)	Map 3
4: Irony Creek (Shuttleworth Bight) to Laura Creek, 23.8–36.1 km (14.8–22.4 mi)	Map 4
5: Laura Creek to Nissen Bight, 36.1–43.1 km (22.4–26.8 mi)	Map 5
6: Nissen Bight to Nels Bight, 43.1–44.8 km (26.8–27.8 mi) to the junction; 0–3.8 km (0–2.4 mi) from the junction to Nels Bight	Map 5
7: Nels Bight to Cape Scott lighthouse (including Guise Bay and Experiment Bight), 3.8–10.4 km (2.4–6.5 mi)	Map 6
8: Nels Bight to San Josef/Cape Scott trailhead, 3.8–0 km (2.4–0) to the junction; 44.8–57.6 km (27.8–35.8 mi)	Maps 6 and 7
9: San Josef/Cape Scott trailhead to San Josef Bay, 0–2.5 km (0–1.6 mi)	Maps 7 and 8
10: San Josef Bay to Mount St. Patrick and Lowrie Bay, 2.5–10.4 km (1.6 –6.5 mi)	Map 8

TRAIL CHAPTERS ARE ORGANIZED according to what this author believes is an ideal trip itinerary from east to west. Of course, how you hike the trail is entirely up to you and will depend on your own pace and logistics. Many may choose to hike the trail in the opposite direction—west to east, starting from San Josef/Cape Scott Trailhead and ending at Shushartie Bay. For this purpose, an abbreviated west to east version of the trail descriptions is provided at the end of this chapter.

TIME AND DISTANCES BETWEEN CAMPSITES

The following are estimated times and will vary depending on weather, trail conditions and personal fitness.

NORTH COAST TRAIL: SHUSHARTIE BAY TRAILHEAD TO NISSEN BIGHT (East to West)

West   East

43.1 km · Nissen Bight	36.1 km · Laura Creek	23.8 km · Irony Creek (Shuttleworth Bight)	16.6 km · Cape Sutil	11.0 km · Nahwitti Campsite	8.7 km · Skinner Creek	0 km · Shushartie Bay
	3–5 hrs 7.0 km	4–8 hrs 12.3 km	4–6 hrs 7.2 km	6–8.5 hrs 5.6 km	1–1.5 hrs 2.3 km	5–7 hrs 8.7 km

CAPE SCOTT TRAILS: SAN JOSEF/CAPE SCOTT TRAILHEAD TO CAPE SCOTT LIGHTHOUSE (South to North)

North   South

23.2 km · Cape Scott Lighthouse	20.7 km · Guise Bay	16.6 km · Nels Bight	12.8 km · Junction	9.6 km · Fisherman River	2.9 km · Eric Lake	0 km · San Josef/ Cape Scott Trailhead
	1 hr 2.5 km	1.5 hrs 4.1 km	1.5 hrs 3.8 km	1–1.5 hrs 3.2 km	2–2.5 hrs 6.7 km	1–1.5 hrs 2.9 km

A FEW IMPORTANT POINTS
ABOUT THE TRAIL DESCRIPTIONS

- For UTM coordinates of water sources, campsites, and beach access points, see page 223.
- Consider beach morphology—the look and feel of beaches are significantly affected by both tidal height and seasonal tidal changes. Best efforts have been made to describe with the highest accuracy possible, but be aware that beaches can change over time. Related to this, buoys marking the forest trails from the beach may move or be blown down.
- One of the primary interests of backpackers is accessible water sources. In addition to the UTM coordinates, best water sources are identified in the text and in the maps. If hiking at the end of the summer, when conditions are dry, understand that these sources may be seasonal and, therefore, unavailable. When in doubt, the official campsites (with the exception of Shushartie Bay) all have reliable water.

ELEVATION PROFILE
SHUSHARTIE BAY TO SAN JOSEF/CAPE SCOTT TRAILHEAD

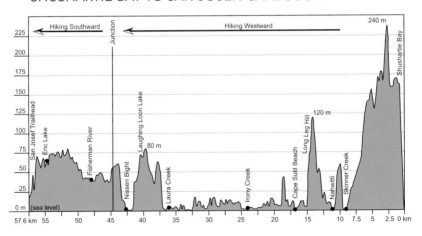

TRAIL SECTION 1

SHUSHARTIE BAY TO SKINNER CREEK
Map 1 — 0–8.7 km (5.4 mi)

OCEAN WAVES BOOKEND THIS exclusively inland section that takes you through a unique upland bog.

HIKING TIME: 5–7 hours

DISTANCE: 8.7 km (around 5.4 mi)

DIFFICULTY: Moderate to difficult

TERRAIN: Exclusively inland. While neither scenic nor easy, this terrain offers an opportunity to pass through a unique upland bog ecosystem. The trail takes you from the ocean to a 247 m (810 ft) plateau and back to sea level. Expect extensive boardwalks, stepladders, ropes, mud, and rugged sections.

HIGHLIGHTS: Whale and wildlife-watching on the water taxi, Shushartie Bay and the estuary, the upland bog ecosystem, Skinner Creek beach, and coastal views to Hope Island.

	SPECIAL CONSIDERATIONS
🚌	Transportation logistics. Must arrange water taxi pick-up/drop-off.
☆	Trailhead
💧	Limited drinking water until Skinner Creek. Pack it in.
☁	Weather conditions affect the difficulty and time to complete this route.
⚠	Challenging terrain. This section can be very muddy and slippery, and offers limited shelter on the upland plateau.

Beach at Shushartie Bay.

SHUSHARTIE BAY, THE EAST trailhead of the North Coast Trail, greets visitors with brooding silence and isolation. Upon your arrival, take a moment to forget that heavy pack and gulp the salty air. Despite rain, sleep deprivation, or forgotten gear, you've made it to one of the most special places on BC's west coast. There is something about being here that makes the heart swell in anticipation and celebration. And with no cell phone access, you are left simply with the here and now. For the next few days, there is nowhere else to be.

The introduction to the North Coast Trail is not a gentle one. Indeed, some consider the Shushartie Bay to Skinner Creek section the most difficult part of the trail. Few would consider it a highlight of their trip (morale-sucking mud and first-day muscle strains might play a role). This section is also exclusively inland—while this is the North Coast Trail, your $10 nightly park fee doesn't get you all coast, all the time. But rest assured: you will see many pretty areas along this route, including 250-year-old trees, giant beds of moss, ferns, dense rainforest, and the unique ecosystem of the upland bogs. Eventually the boggy plateau gives

Trailhead sign at Shushartie Bay.

way to rainforest and descends through ancient cedars, spruce, salal, and huckleberry to greet the salt air of the ocean. The beach at Skinner Creek campsite is a fantastic reward.

 The northern trailhead at Shushartie Bay is marine access only. While old logging roads once made it possible to hike into Shushartie Bay, the route is not maintained and Park Facility Operators discourage this route to minimize encounters with black bears. Reserve the water taxi for its morning departure from Port Hardy. The 45-minute ride doubles as a wildlife-viewing adventure—keep an eye out for breaching whales, porpoises, jumping fish, seals, sea otters, sea lions, and birds. From the water taxi, hikers have even spotted wolves swimming in pursuit of deer! After passing Nigei Island on your right, Shushartie Bay suddenly appears.

As the water taxi cuts its engine and sputters into the stillness of Shushartie Bay, it is nearly impossible not to feel like an intruder. Even colourful hiking clothes seem too loud. Take a moment to imagine this place more than two centuries ago when it was a bustling trade centre for sea otter pelts and other furs. Protected by a curving coastline and watchful islands, the bay provided a natural landing spot for First Nations and European traders. Now, with the exception of logging on the eastern hillsides, nature has reclaimed this place.

Quiet as it may be, Shushartie Bay is very much alive. Fed by the Shushartie River and mixing tides, the kilometre-wide estuary offers rich habitat for wildlife. Black bears forage here frequently so take precautions to avoid bear encounters.

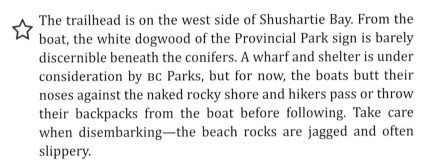

The trailhead is on the west side of Shushartie Bay. From the boat, the white dogwood of the Provincial Park sign is barely discernible beneath the conifers. A wharf and shelter is under consideration by BC Parks, but for now, the boats butt their noses against the naked rocky shore and hikers pass or throw their backpacks from the boat before following. Take care when disembarking—the beach rocks are jagged and often slippery.

The route from Shushartie Bay to Skinner Creek is one of two major inland sections of the North Coast Trail. It does not begin gently. Say farewell to the coast for now and head in and up. From the beach, the trail immediately climbs a steep, burnt-out hillside. In 2010, a fire charred the forest and damaged the trail, making it rough, loose, and treacherous. Fortunately, the trail has since been rerouted to make it safer.

SHUSHARTIE BAY CAMPSITE

APPROXIMATELY 50 M (AROUND 164 ft) up the trail lies the Shushartie Bay campsite, nestled in the shade of old-growth

💧 **WATER IS LIMITED** at the Shushartie Bay campsite so be sure to pack in drinking water if you plan to stay the night. A freshwater waterfall exists two beaches to the northwest. However, it is only accessible during low tide. Pack in water for your hike to Skinner Creek as there are only low-quality sources en route.

hemlock and Sitka spruce (some over 250 years old). The site provides four tent pads, a food locker, and an outhouse. In 2014, a new shelter with a cooking area and benches was installed at Shushartie Bay. Since the water taxi is a morning drop-off, you will likely bypass the Shushartie Bay campsite unless you are hiking the trail west and plan to be picked up there. Situated high on the hillside under the protective cover of trees, it is a dark campsite. The estuary can be glimpsed below, and if you listen, you'll likely hear the scramble of bears walking on the rocky shore below. It may not be scenic, but the mystic perch of Shushartie Bay rivals that of any Star Wars Ewok village.

From the campsite, the trail continues up the hillside through dense second-growth forest. With full packs and still-waking muscles, the first hour is one of the toughest and will have you huffing. Ropes help you on the climb where needed and the

Stairs on the trail.

Boardwalk at upland bog. *Photo: Andrew Bruce Lau*

uphill slog will even out. Once you gain the plateau, the hardest part will be over.

Common vegetation includes salal, huckleberries, deer fern, lily of the valley, mosses, yellow cedar, lodgepole pine, and western hemlock. About 300 m (984 ft) from the trailhead, a clearing in the forest provides a decent glimpse of Goletas Channel, Shushartie Bay, and the east hillside, part of which has been recently logged. Here, you have already gained 175 m (about 574 ft) in elevation! More rope work lies ahead, but you can expect a gentler incline and only mild undulations as you head inland towards the plateau.

Just over an hour from here you will encounter the first sections of boardwalk—substantial stretches of sun-bleached platforms snaking through the landscape. Where you don't find boardwalk, you will probably find oozing mud, pooling, and sucking. Despite this, it should be steady going with an occasional rope or set of wooden steps to help you in the trickiest places. Watch your footwork—stumps, roots, and rocks dot the trail and trip the tired or inattentive hiker.

As you reach the plateau, forest gives way to sky and an upland bog. This unique ecosystem provides important habitat to amphibians, invertebrates, birds, and fragile vegetation. Similar to alpine environments, the upland bog is simultaneously tough but delicate. Stunted trees, grassy meadows, and tangled shrubs give it a muskeg-like appearance. While this environment can withstand exposure, torrential downpour, and hurricane-force winds, it is not so resilient to human footsteps. Expertly constructed boardwalk prevents damage over the wettest parts of the bog but where the trail is raw, avoid widening it further. Remember that you can take off your boots at the end of the day, but the ground will wear your boot prints for the rest of the year, if not longer.

You will reach the "summit" (247 m or around 810 ft) of this section after about two hours of moderate hiking from the trailhead (there is no marker). From here, the trail gradually descends. Expect stepladders, sturdy beams laid across the mud, and nylon rope for climbing or descending. Tramping along extensive stretches of boardwalk may lull you into inattentiveness but keep your eyes open for a small sign on the ground marking the halfway point at 4.3 km (about 2.7 mi). In clear weather, this area of boardwalk makes one of the better break points in this section. Take a moment to enjoy the quiet where even birds rarely sing.

The second half of the trail is easy going with the exception of more mud. In some places you'll be wallowing knee-deep. Pass over the last of the boardwalk and the trail begins descending through salal, huckleberries, and big cedars.

You will likely hear the rush and smell the salty air before you actually see the ocean. A final staircase leads down almost to the bed of Skinner Creek. Skinner Creek is shallow but has a wide creek bed full of river rock—an indication of powerful volumes in the winter season. To access the beach and camping area, cross the shallow creek or (more awkwardly) scramble over or under the huge stack of blown-down trees that lies perpendicular to the creek. Fierce winter storms and flooding have resulted in upheavals, disintegrations, or extensive reorganizations of the creek and riverbed. At Skinner Creek, the stack of blown-down trees continues to grow. As of 2011, some downed logs had steps cut into them to help hikers clamber over. How long—or in what direction—these steps will remain before nature shifts the logs, nobody knows.

SKINNER CREEK CAMPSITE

THE BEACH AT SKINNER Creek is peaceful. Its wide, expansive stretch of sand and pebbles is a relief after the mud and shadows of the forest. Across Goletas Channel you can see Hope Island and with a clear sky, Mount Waddington and the Coastal Range

Beach at Skinner Creek, looking east. *Photo: Andrew Bruce Lau*

mountains. Shed your pack, relax to the sound of waves rolling continuously up and back down the tidal edge. From Skinner Creek, many people decide to gain a couple of extra kilometres and push on to Nahwitti River (a further 11 km, or around 6.8 mi). If you stay at Skinner Creek, you will probably arrive with enough time to relax, beach walk, read, and cook before bed.

Camping at Skinner Creek is best on the beach, with the sandy bar east of the creek providing the ideal spot. Really though, almost anywhere above high tide will do. At the forest edge on the southwest side of the river, you will find the BC Parks sign and map. Just beyond are the fire pit, food locker, and outhouse. In rough weather, only a couple of tents will fit under the shelter of the tree canopy. Be conscious of wildlife here—use the food locker and keep a meticulously clean site. As much as this beach site makes a great human camp, it is even more popular with the locals, as evidenced by prolific tracks from bear, wolf, cougar, and deer.

MERMAID'S PURSE (also called a devil's purse) is the casing that surrounds the fertilized eggs of sharks, skates, and chimaeras. Walking along the beaches of the North Coast Trail, you are likely to find these mysterious seaweed-coloured casings washed ashore. Lightweight and buoyant, the casings often lie at the strandline, the farthest point of the high tide. The egg cases that wash up on beaches are usually empty, the young fish having already hatched out. *Photo: Andrew Bruce Lau*

Skinner Creek with Hope Island in the distance. *Photo: Andrew Bruce Lau*

Water is easily accessible and of good quality at Skinner Creek. However, seagulls congregate where the creek flows onto the beach, and their main hobbies are bathing, pooping, and preening directly in the creek. Pull your water well away from the gull zone, and keep your own food scraps and pollution out of the creek.

THE OCEAN AT THIS section of beach is not recommended for swimming. The angle of the beach creates forceful wave action, and there is a steep, strong undercurrent. Find safer conditions at the west end of the beach, but use your best judgment.

Skinner Creek's beach provides a fantastic chance to spot marine wildlife. Porpoises, sea lions, and even whales frequently use this marine passageway on their mysterious journeys. Discover sea stars and mermaid's purses washed ashore, or wander to the far east side of the beach where the rock formations, exciting headlands, and surge channels are more than worth a visit. At nightfall, you may hear the lonely call of the lighthouse at Nahwitti Bar across the water, warning marine craft of dangerous standing waves.

TRAIL SECTION 2

SKINNER CREEK TO NAHWITTI RIVER
AND CAPE SUTIL
Map 2 — 8.7–16.6 km (5.4–10.3 mi)

AS TOUGH AND RUGGED as it is beautiful, this route provides a mix of forest and beach hiking that culminates at the northern-most tip of Vancouver Island.

HIKING TIME: 5–7 hours

DISTANCE: 7.9 km (around 4.9 mi), 2.3 km (around 1.4 mi) to Nahwitti River

DIFFICULTY: Difficult to very difficult

TERRAIN: Forest and beach hiking. Expect flat terrain through old-growth trees at Nahwitti River, then a cable car crossing, followed by rough, steep sections, and rope work. The final approach to Sutil is interspersed with several pocket beaches laden with cobblestones.

HIGHLIGHTS: Historic settlement sites, the Nahwitti River and forest, Long Leg Hill staircase, Tripod Beach, and Cape Sutil—the most northern tip of Vancouver Island.

THROUGH CURTAINS OF RAIN or dazzling sunshine, the coast is always there. Views in this section serve as a reminder of where you have come from and tempt you with the promise of more ahead. There is also the exciting geographical milestone of the most northern tip of Vancouver Island, and your destination: Cape Sutil. Now, several kilometres into your journey, you are delving deeper into the heart of the North Coast Trail. The trail from Skinner Creek to Cape Sutil travels through ancient forests

SPECIAL CONSIDERATIONS	
⬆	Alternate routes from Skinner Creek beach.
⚠	Challenging terrain, particularly on the approach to Cape Sutil. Expect rope rappels down steep, slippery slopes.
⛔	Impassible headland/high tide zones. Tide tables are strongly recommended for this section in two key areas: *West Skinner Creek beach:* Very high tide can affect the beach route, particularly in winter. Some streams flow underneath the sand and, on rare occasions, high tide coincides with higher stream flows, making this area unsafe to cross. An alternative route is available. *Tripod Beach:* This beach, at the bottom of Long Leg Hill, is impassable at high tide.

and sacred places. Beaches greet you with wide-open solitude. There is no better way to feel alive.

It is important to time this section well to avoid impassible high-tide parts. Read your tide tables and plan your hike to avoid two key pinch points. The most important of these is

Heading west on the Skinner Creek beach. *Photo: Andrew Bruce Lau*

I only went out for a walk and finally concluded to stay out till sundown, for going out, I found, was really going in.
—JOHN MUIR, 1913

near Tripod Beach at the base of Long Leg Hill, where you can be trapped for hours if you do not time it well. You do not want to be doing the final leg—a very rugged route to Cape Sutil—in the dark. The west side of the Skinner Creek beach is also inaccessible at extremely high tides.

There are some fairly rough and technically challenging sections that will tire out even the fittest hiker. A few easy forest sections provide relief but, in general, expect ruggedness, significant mud, high steps up and over stumps and logs, and several steep climbs with lots of rope work, including the beach accesses. But this section is not without its rewards—there are magnificent forests, hidden pocket beaches and, if you look closely, wildlife. Cape Sutil provides an excellent place for a well-earned rest.

SKINNER CREEK TO NAHWITTI RIVER CAMPSITE

The hike from Skinner Creek to Nahwitti River campsite takes 60–90 minutes. Heading west, you have two options for the initial route—forest or beach. Most choose the slightly faster and easier beach route. At the end of the beach is an impassible headland, but a forest trail (marked by buoys) goes up a steep, rope-assisted trail, and around this obstacle. However, when tides are very high or there is significant stream flow (usually just in the winter), the beach route can be dangerous or impassable. Access to the forest route is via a trail behind the outhouse

Picnic on the idyllic Nahwitti River.

at Skinner Creek. While it lacks the scenic view of the beach route, and is a bit rougher, the forest route has two points of interest. Remnants of an old cabin are right beside the trail, including framing, an old stove, and dishes. The other feature is a unique sub-surface stream bed.

THE TWO ROUTES JOIN in the forest and the remainder of the hiking to the Nahwitti River campsite is relatively easy. Expect sturdy ladders, ropes, and roots, but not much muck. Pay attention to the terrain—about 40 minutes from Skinner Creek, the trail begins to follow parts of the old settler's corduroy road, slightly overgrown and uneven but resiliently intact about 100 years after its construction. Before long, the trail emerges from the forest onto a steep cobblestone beach at the edge of a little bay.

The Nahwitti River campsite, located at kilometre 11 (mile 6.8) of the North Coast Trail, is just down the beach, marked by buoys and a hand-carved sign. The campsite itself is tucked in the trees just off from what can be a windy beach. There is a BC Parks sign, a map, a food locker, and four tent pads. While not as scenic as Skinner Creek, the Nahwitti campsite is definitely comfortable and often preferred by those on a more aggressive schedule. Just west of the campsite is a sandbar and the river mouth. The estuary is a common site for bears and sea birds. Historically, the Nahwitti River was a popular spot—at one time it was the site of a First Nations village, and later a European settlement site. On the opposite side of the river mouth from the campsite are old cabins said to have been used by US president Theodore Roosevelt for hunting and fishing.

Water is taken from the Nahwitti River itself. At low tide, you can get water from anywhere along the river. But at high tide, hike upstream to about three-quarters of the way to the cable car to avoid the tidal mixing. If you continue on the trail, consider holding out for a better water source on the west side of Nahwitti River, about 1 km (around 0.6 mi) from the cable car.

NAHWITTI RIVER TO CAPE SUTIL

FROM THE NAHWITTI RIVER campsite, follow the trail along the river to the cable car. Nahwitti River is idyllic. After thousands of years of quiet meandering, the river has created its own picturesque valley bottom—a meadow-like stopping place for many waterfowl and songbirds.

The trail along the river is peaceful, flat, and easy. Hemlock dominates the forest, and their acidic needles have created tough competition for other vegetation. The resulting terrain is deep, loamy, and gentle on the knees. Ancient stumps are ever so slowly returning to the earth, and nurse logs support the next generation.

HOW TO RIDE A CABLE CAR WITH STYLE

Only two people should use the cable car at once.

Use caution when entering and exiting. One person should stabilize the car as the other loads your backpacks before holding the rope firmly as the first person steps in.

Let gravity carry the car to the middle of the line, then as the car begins to slow, start pulling the rope towards the other side. Pace yourself, and smile as you feel your biceps burn.

Some recommend wearing gloves for the rope pulling. Whether you use them or not, gloves are never a bad idea to have on a hiking trip.

Be nice—if a solo hiker is travelling behind you, send the car back to the other side to help them.

Passing through this beautiful space, it is easy to feel like a passer-by—just a humble blink in the memory of a very old place.

At this point of the trail, you'll see the cable car to cross the river. At the sight of it, you can't help but be excited—50 m (about 165 ft) of zip-line style fun. Shouldn't there be a line-up? Your hiking buddy is likely already clambering up the stairs to the launching platform. In the narrow steel box, make sure you grip the platform until you and your partner are *both* ready to go. And then let go. The first part of the ride is five seconds of child-like bliss as the car gathers speed and whips through the air. The second part is three minutes of arm-burning exhaustion as you work to pull the metal car the rest of the way across the river to the opposite platform. If you prefer to avoid the cable car, Nahwitti River may be shallow enough to ford, dependent on season and weather. Be careful of slippery river rocks and unbuckle your pack for a fast escape if you fall into the water.

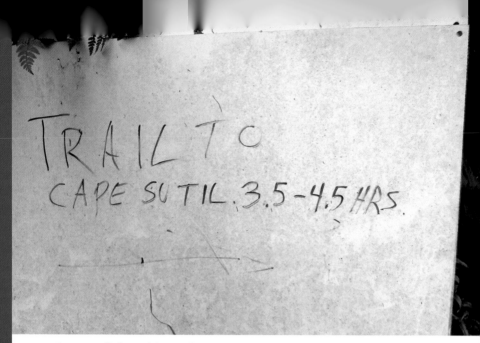

Getting off the cable car, find a high-budget sign—only around 4 hours of hiking to Cape Sutil.

From the cable car, expect approximately 3 km (around 1.9 mi) of forest hiking before you reach the first pocket beach. The trail takes you through a small meadow and (mostly) dry riverbed. It then passes through a small, dense stand of trees before climbing slightly away from the riverbed. About 1 km (around 0.6 mi) from the cable car is a small creek that provides a good water source (see Map 2 or page 223 for UTM coordinates). From here, the trail climbs into a stunning hemlock grove, blazing green down the hillside—a definite highlight of this section of the trail. Before long, you will arrive at the first of several cobblestone beaches and rocky headlands. Keep an eye out for buoys marking the re-entry to the forest. These beach sections are short, but offer fantastic views of the shoreline to the east and west, including Cape Sutil. If the tide is low, this is a great opportunity to explore the rich intertidal life along the rocks and in the tide pools.

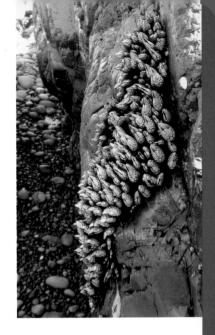

Gooseneck barnacles exposed at low tide. These filter-feeding crustaceans live attached to rocks in the intertidal zone.

⊖ The last stretch to Cape Sutil is marked by Long Leg Hill and an impassable high tide section near Tripod Beach at kilometre 16 (around mile 10). More than 250 steps lead down to a smooth-stone beach and a beautiful section of black basalt outcrops, with caves and archways (includ-ing the "tripod" that the beach is named for) carved out over thousands of years by the churning surf. If you haven't timed it right, high tide makes it impossible to get by this rocky section. Do not wade into the ocean to get across—the waves are strong and can pummel you against the rocks or sweep you out to sea. If camping becomes necessary, the east side of this beach pro-vides room for a tent, and there is space in the forest at the top of the stairs for one or two tents. Water access is on the beach about 50 m (164 ft) west from the base of the staircase (see map on page 123).

⚠ The final approach to Cape Sutil can be intimidating and re-quires careful hiking. With the help of rope, you will climb up a steep hill, only to come to a thin ridge that leads directly down again. The descent is much less stable—more of a clay bank than a trail—and you must take a strong hold of the rope and walk/belay your way down. It can be slippery in the rain. In the future, this area may have ladders installed, but for now, use caution and confidence.

A good example of some of the rope climbs and rappels to be expected on the North Coast Trail.

CAPE SUTIL

THE CAPE SUTIL CAMPSITE is located at kilometre 16.6 (mile 10.3). A small bay calms the water and on a blue-sky day, it feels as though you've found a secret west coast oasis. With the exception of the cape itself, which is a First Nations reserve of the Nahwitti, you are now on the most northern tip of Vancouver Island!

Cape Sutil makes a great campsite for many reasons. The sandy beach stretches just under a kilometre (about half a mile) long and there are several places to pitch a tent above the high tide line. There is no forest camping, but the bay is sheltered from extreme weather and there are enough tree overhangs on the beach to construct a good tarp shelter in the likely event of pounding rain. Cape Sutil is also the location of the ranger station—a semi-permanent yurt tucked in the forest. A beacon of civilization, the yurt discharges friendly Park Facility Officers

THE YURT AT CAPE SUTIL is used as a base camp for park maintenance and operations. It is occupied from May 15 to September 30. At other times of the year, it is available to the public for emergency use. If you do use it, please leave it in good condition.

who may share some interesting facts about the area, provide some tips on the route ahead, or even play a game of bocce with you. The food locker and outhouse are located under the forest canopy at the west side of the beach. The outhouse is about 75 m (around 246 ft) down the trail and has a guestbook to record your experience.

Potable water is a little way from the main camp area, about 100 m (328 ft) east of the food locker. Walk along the beach until you spot a path in the forest that leads to the creek. Prior to this path, water was seasonal and accessed from a pit dug in the sand by the park rangers.

Cape Sutil is culturally significant and should be respected. Formerly the principal village site of the Nahwitti First Nations, it was shelled and burned by the British naval fleet in 1850 and 1851. The villagers fled and many of them relocated to Hope

Late arrival: approaching Cape Sutil as night and rain set in.
Photo: Andrew Bruce Lau

Island (see page 151 for more about this). Today, the northern tip of the cape is a reserve of the Nahwitti First Nation and should not be trespassed upon. The reserve boundary starts right around the outcropping of rocks at the centre of the north beach (a rocky headland separates the main beach from this beach). Beach camping is allowed on the north beach and there is a trail over the headland that provides access. However, this trail is not maintained by BC Parks as it would make the reserve more accessible and trespassing more likely.

OTHER NOTES FROM CAPE SUTIL

· There is good swimming here, if you can handle the cold.

· Fishing from the beach is possible, but make sure you have the right licence.

· There is wildlife to be spotted—keep an eye out for wolf and other animal tracks, and look out to the ocean to see sea birds, seals, and jumping salmon.

TRAIL SECTION 3

CAPE SUTIL TO IRONY CREEK
(SHUTTLEWORTH BIGHT)
Map 3 — 16.6–23.8 km (10.3–14.8 mi)

THE HEART OF THE North Coast Trail is wild, dramatic, and mostly coastal.

HIKING TIME: 4–6 hours

DISTANCE: 7.2 km (around 4.5 mi)

DIFFICULTY: Difficult

TERRAIN: Primarily cobblestone beaches connected by short inland trails. Expect steep scrambles and climbs.

HIGHLIGHTS: Beautiful coastline views and extensive beach walking, rocky headlands, and pocket beaches. The tombolo, expansive and sandy Shuttleworth Bight, wolves, seabirds, and other wildlife.

	SPECIAL CONSIDERATIONS
⬆	Alternate route. Take the alternate inland routes only during very high tides or inclement weather as it is more difficult and less scenic than the beach.
⊖	Impassible headlands/high tide zone.
💧	Water sources noted along this section should be considered seasonal. The most reliable sources are at Cape Sutil, just west of the tombolo and Irony Creek.

A TICKET TO ANY sunny destination in the world can offer you warm sand and garnished cocktails, but it can't get you this. Along this route are some of the most exotic, scenic beaches on

Storm, sand and surf. A classic North Coast beach (about 20 minutes west of the tombolo).

Vancouver Island. Standing on the beach, between forest and sea, you are confronted with an overwhelming vastness—you can't help but feel on the edge of the world.

From Cape Sutil, the trail heads west, gradually taking you south towards the long sandy swoop of Shuttleworth Bight. Most of this route traces the shoreline. You will leave your tracks in the sand next to those of the wolves.

Many short inland sections cut through dense rainforest jungles to avoid rough, impassible headlands. On these sections, keep an eye out for culturally modified trees. Culturally modified trees (CMTs) are trees modified by indigenous people as part of their traditional use of the forest. The most popular species used is western red cedar and modifications include bark stripping, chopping for pitch, plank removal, and de-limbing for wood. If you encounter a CMT, do not damage or move it, or impact the site—it may be protected under the *Heritage Conservation Act.*

On the forest trails expect difficult scrambles and steep climbs with occasional ocean views where the canopy clears. The forest trails along this section represent true west coast rainforest. The underbrush is thick with ferns and tangled salal, which thrive on slowly deteriorating nurse logs. You'll see cedar, hemlock, fir, and spruce, as well as lichen and moss.

ALONG THIS SECTION, TIDES and geography allow for mostly coastal hiking, with many short inland sections (little more than 5 minutes each) and a couple longer ones.

Depart Cape Sutil by following the path in the woods towards the outhouse. The trail continues for about 15 minutes, taking you across the cape to the first of many beaches along this section. Here, sandy areas amidst cobblestones, make it possible to camp on the exposed northeast side. Water is accessed from a seasonal stream that runs under the rocks just before the next overland heading west. Find it by going up into the salal.

At the end of this first beach, a short connecting trail takes you through the forest to the second beach—a beautiful bay about 225 m (around 750 ft) long. The terrain is pebbles, cobblestones, and jumbled driftwood. Beds of kelp and whale-like chunks of black basalt nestle close to the shore. Watch for the real thing too—orcas have been spotted off the coast of this beach. At the end of the beach, a snag with colourful buoys hanging from it marks the trail back into the forest for another short inland section (5 minutes).

About 30 minutes, or just under 2 km (1.2 mi) from Cape Sutil, you come to a junction in the forest. To the right, a cleft in the rock provides a view down to the beach. To the left, continues an alternate inland trail (best avoided on all but the highest tides). The next half kilometre has both beach and alternate

65

inland trail with several access points (see inset map). Stay on the beach unless high tide forces you inland; the coastal route is easier and more scenic.

Along the beach, if tides permit, you will be able to travel along a 450-m (1,480-ft) rocky shoreline before the forest trail resumes. Several headlands along this section of beach are impassable at high tide. The route should be fairly obvious—when high tides or headlands make for impassable sections, you will be forced to leave the beach and take the forest trail. If needed, three access points (scrambles!) marked by buoys provide a way up to the alternate inland route. At the very highest tides, you must take the first trail access, or expect to backtrack when stopped by a barrier of rock and crashing waves. But, if tides permit, you will be able to squeeze along the rock and the waves without getting wet.

At the end of this beach, a gap in the rock leads back up into the forest where a short trail connects you to another beach (the alternate inland route also merges at this point). After crossing this second beach, you re-enter the forest and begin one of the two larger overland portions of the trail between

Tombolo in the distance, 2 hours west of Sutil. *Photo: Andrew Bruce Lau*

Sutil and Irony Creek. This forested section takes approximate-ly 30 minutes and follows the coast closely but at a higher eleva-tion. The trail is undulating with mud, roots, and several steep climbs. Now-familiar nylon rope snakes down the steepest sec-tions and provides helpful handholds where you need it most. Watch for wildlife, especially the quiet and delicate amphibians underfoot. Tough as the trail may be, the forest feels enchanted. On this forest trail, you find a Medusa-looking cedar—several heads and unruly serpentine branches sprout from a single trunk. Next to it is a simple bench that (apart from outhouse thrones) is the only human-constructed rest stop on the trail. Take a break to enjoy the calm of these forest groves. As you gain elevation, views of the coast emerge.

Water is available from several seasonal sources along this sec-tion (see the map or page 223 for UTM coordinates for exact locations). The best option is in the forest, at about kilometre 19 following the medusa cedar. If hiking early in the summer, this enthusiastic stream is hard to miss—cold, clear water running right beside the trail.

SHORTLY AFTER THIS, YOU leave the forest and begin a kilome-tre-long (around 0.6 mi) stretch of easy, pebbly terrain. This section of coastline is divided by a forested headland and short connector trail marked by buoys. Camping is possible here, but a lack of water and an uncomfortable slope make it not ideal.

In the distance is the tombolo. From afar, it looks like just another rocky bluff topped with a patch of conifers. But at the end of the beach, a short bridle trail through grass and salal takes you over a spit and to a stunning surprise: a wild-looking bay where powerful waves hit jagged rock with such force that sea spray is sent, again and again, into the air. To your right, the curve of the sandbar and the "island" (a rocky bluff) form the tombolo. The landscape tells a story of frequent storms and

WHAT IS A TOMBOLO?

A tombolo is a spit or sandbar that connects an island to the mainland. They are formed by wave refraction—as the waves bend around the outlying island (and laterally along the shoreline) they carry sediment with them. When enough sediment accumulates, it forms a spit.

endless surf. Jumbles of driftwood are strewn on the spit and windswept trees hang on tenaciously.

The tombolo is located at kilometre 20 (around mile 12.4), just over 3 km (around 2 mi) from Cape Sutil. From the tombolo, the trail runs along the rocky, windblown bay and enters a section of open forest with ocean views. From this point, the coastline and trail arc southward. The trail avoids a major rocky headland and, instead cuts through a challenging section of forest. Around 20 minutes west of the tombolo, you arrive at a gorgeous beach of cobblestones and toe-tempting sand. If the weather is good, this beach makes a great halfway break. The view to the west is stunning—a raw, unforgiving, and isolated landscape of waves, wind, and rain. The trail ahead to Shuttleworth Bight is almost exclusively beach. At a moderate pace, with time to enjoy views and do a little beachcombing, it takes about 3 hours to reach Irony Creek campsite from this beach.

There are a series of stunning beaches along this section, each with its own unique shape and texture. Soft and loamy sand, pebbles, and beach rock are the dominant landscape. Large cobblestones, endless piles of driftwood, and steeply sloped, uneven terrain motivate weary hikers to press on for kinder ground. While your heart will be full with the breathtaking scenery, your feet will likely ache by day's end. To make your hike easier, look for flat, rocky shelves and the cushiony spring offered by massive beds of seaweed.

The coast is an obvious wildlife haven. It is not only important as a natural travel corridor but also for hunting and foraging. In the earlier part of the summer, eagles nest and feed here in prolific numbers. You can spot their massive nests in high snags overlooking their marine kitchen. Keep a lookout for timid seabirds at the surf's edge or resting on the rocky outcrops. In the sand you can spot a variety of animal tracks—from deer, bears, and elusive wolves.

Within a kilometre (around 0.6 mi) of Irony Creek, there are a couple sandy areas that, with a little levelling, would make a good site to pitch a tent. But with no water source, push on if you can. Camping on Shuttleworth Bight at Irony Creek is a treat. As you arrive, you must first cross Irony Creek itself to access the campsites on the west side. Balance along the driftwood logs or ford the creek at the shallower section on the beach. Be careful here, as both the logs and the rocks can be slippery, and early in the season or after a heavy rainfall the creek can be strong.

Irony Creek campsite is located just off the beach under shelter of Sitka and hemlock fir. It has all the amenities of a five-star backcountry campsite: easy water access from Irony Creek, forest shelter, four tent pads, an outhouse, and a food locker. Shuttleworth Bight, the nearly 2-km (around 1.2-mi) long sandy bay, provides additional beach camping above high tide, although the driest spaces are located a decent

Wolf tracks on the beach (near the remains of a very fresh deer kill).

69

Sunset at Shuttleworth Bight.

walk away from the food lockers and water. If you can, locate your camp on the east side of the Bight as there are no suitable food locker options (trees, lockers, or otherwise) on the west end.

Swimming is excellent here. As usual on this coast, be cautious of rip currents, high waves, and stay close to shore. Surfers also use this beach.

Shuttleworth Bight is a welcome sandy respite for tired hikers. Find a patch of beach to relax on and watch the tireless waves where sea lions jump. Thousands of limpets lie scattered by the tide, and fantastic cloud patterns paint the sky. You'll see wolf tracks and, if you're lucky, the wolves themselves. Take off your bag and enjoy watching the day fall away.

TRAIL SECTION 4

IRONY CREEK (SHUTTLEWORTH BIGHT)
TO LAURA CREEK
Map 4 — 23.8–36.1 km (14.8–22.4 mi)

KEEP YOUR HEAD UP to take in the beauty of the coast—this section can be an exhausting slog over uncountable cobblestones.

HIKING TIME: 5–7 hours
DISTANCE: 12.3 km (7.6 mi)
DIFFICULTY: Difficult
TERRAIN: Predominantly beach hiking interspersed with some forest. Beach terrain is tough with many cobblestones.
HIGHLIGHTS: Beautiful Shuttleworth Bight, the Strandby River cable car, and forested riverbed. On the beach come across animal tracks and interesting debris (bones, seabirds, eagle nests, etc.).

	SPECIAL CONSIDERATIONS
⚠	Challenging terrain due to cobblestones and sloped beaches. If the tide is up, the terrain will be more difficult and, therefore, more time intensive.
	Limited camping opportunities at Laura Creek.
	Unofficial camping opportunities.

DRINKING WATER AT STRANDBY RIVER

Avoid pulling water from Strandby River. Even at the cable car crossing, tidal mixing makes for a salty drink. Instead, an excellent water source lies about 1 km (around 0.6 mi) west of the cable car crossing. A small and usually swift stream runs across the trail. It can sometimes slow to a mild trickle, depending on summer conditions. If this is the case, you can follow it about 3 m (around 10 ft) off the trail and towards the marsh, where it falls over a small drop.

MILLIONS OF COBBLESTONES AWAIT you along this section, laid upon seemingly endless miles of unsteady terrain. Expansive coastal views and wildlife viewing opportunities are your reward on this mostly coastal section of trail from Shuttleworth Bight to Laura Creek. The first few kilometres are beautiful and easy, giving your body a chance to warm up and your mind to wander. From the seemingly desolate bight to the moist forest along the Strandby River, life is pervasive, in every driftwood log, cedar canopy, or mossy tuft. In the forest, centipedes, frogs, ferns, and mushrooms create their own universe in miniature. The trail crosses parts of the original settlers' road, where nature is fast taking over. At Strandby River, you will take your second, and final, cable car crossing of the trail.

ON THE BEACHES, BLACK and tan volcanic rocks speak to the ancient history of this area. The terrain is rough-looking with sea stacks and beautiful rock formations. Washed-up marine debris lie scattered on the shore among disorderly piles of driftwood, bones, and empty shells. Dried crusts of dead sea stars and coral skeletons lie alongside. As you amble over cobblestones and

73

thick, loamy beds of seaweed, remember to lift your head to see ravens, eagles, and many different seabirds.

Water access is adequate on this route (see map on page 125). As well as creeks and rivers in the forest, there are several points on the beaches were fresh water rushes out onto the beach from secret creeks and streams, emerging as capillary etchings in the sand.

There are a couple unofficial camping options on this section, with Wolftrack Beach being the best. But don't be misled by the beach terrain—there is very little in the way of comfortable camping options.

If weather is harsh, this section is much more difficult. Most of the trail consists of exposed beach hiking offering little shade from sun or shelter from rain and wind. Do not underestimate the slog of the beach route. Laura Creek provides a nice break but is not the most idyllic campsite on the trail.

AS DIFFICULT AS IT may be to leave Shuttleworth Bight, the departure is lovely. Heading west you will enjoy a full kilometre (around 0.6 mi) of relaxed beach walking. It is easy to get distracted by tidal curiosities—you'll find tangles of bull kelp, colourful shells the size of barley pearls, and other beach wash-up, including persistent plastic and other human-made trash.

TOWARDS THE END OF the beach is the trail access and, about 100 m (around 328 ft) after that, the mouth of the Strandby River. Walk the extra bit along the beach to have a peek at the estuary and wildlife that congregates there. Mergansers, osprey, coots, and other wildfowl are common, attracted to the salmon and other rich food sources that the river estuary provides. The mouth of the river is wide and calm. Large trees flank the river

Cable car at Strandby River. *Photo: Andrew Bruce Lau*

and offer added protection. The Strandby is also one of the only rivers along this section of coast that is deep enough to bring in a skiff for transportation. The European settlers who lived here did this. Today, it provides a potential water taxi drop-off point for hikers.

About three-quarters of the way along Shuttleworth Bight, look for buoys at the forest edge marking the way. From the beach, the trail plunges into the woods and runs alongside the Strandby River to a cable car crossing a few hundred metres in. The terrain is flat and easy. This is a beautiful stretch of old growth, thick with hemlock, spruce, and undergrowth of berry bushes, deer fern, and ubiquitous mosses. Along the riverbed, keep an eye out for signs of the old settlers' road.

The cable car is just before kilometre 26 (mile 16), or about 2 km (around 1.2 mi) from Irony Creek campsite. Depending on how much beachcombing you do, it should take 40–60 minutes to cover this distance. To avoid flooding, bank erosion, and the river's constant meandering, the cable car is situated well up the river at a stable and narrow section. The steel platforms are built high above the river, and the cables stretch like long clotheslines across the shallow section of river. Bright buoys hang alongside, warning low-flying aircraft to steer clear.

Heading west after the cable car, the forest trail resumes and travels roughly parallel to the river as it flows out to sea. As you near the mouth of the river, the trail veers left to avoid another headland. Within 1.5 km (around 0.9 mi) of the cable car you arrive at a small pocket beach. This is the first in a series of north-facing beaches that are connected by several short forest trails.

For the next 2 km (around 1.2 mi), coastal hiking provides a mixed terrain comprising thick mats of seaweed, driftwood, pebbles, some sand and cobblestones. If the tide is right, there are also some excellent tidal pools to explore. Interesting black, tan, and rust-coloured rock distinguishes this area and parts

Wolftrack Beach (or Sunny Bay), looking east. *Photo: Andrew Bruce Lau*

of the beach are limestone. The rust-coloured bands are intrusions of highly mineralized igneous rock.

Use caution and common sense to avoid bear encounters. Remember everywhere along the trail, but especially near the ocean surf where sea life is plentiful, you are in foraging territory for bears.

Rounding a headland, the trail turns southwest. At about kilometre 29.5 (mile 18.3), you come to the best undesignated campsite on the trail: Wolftrack Beach (also called Sunny Bay by many). You know you've reached it when you go over a short, well-trodden overland path and descend down a chunk of rock to a beach about 200 metres (650 ft) long. While unmarked, this beautiful little beach can be distinguished by its soft sand, gently swooping bay and driftwood logs that provide great seating for watching sunsets. Wolftrack Beach can fit a few tents comfortably (you should camp here only if you know how to cache your food independently). At low tide, exposed rock and seaweed frame an idyllic coastal view. To the east is the tip of the forested and grassy crescent from which you've come and to the west, the way ahead juts out like a finger pointing to nowhere. The tip of that "finger" is Christensen Point and, beyond that, you can see your first view of Cape Scott. A seasonal water source is available from a creek located roughly in the centre of the bay beside a couple of large logs. The water flows into the sand, so you will have to go to the forest's edge to collect it. If this is dried up, you can also gather water from beaches to the east or west.

Until now, the terrain has been a mix of pebbles, soft seaweed, and forest trail. After Wolftrack Beach, there are two short inland sections (the first travels along a minor cliff ringing a small bay). Separating them is a small cove with a good water source. Following this, the long and difficult slog on pebble and cobblestone beaches begins. From here, it will take 3–4 hours (about 7 km or 4.3 mi) to reach Laura Creek. This terrain

Christensen Point, looking west with Cape Scott in the distance.

is tiring—aside from the unforgiving rock, there is awkwardly slanting shoreline and giant beds of energy-sucking seaweed to contend with. If tides are in your favour, you may be able to hike on sand or rock platforms in the low-tide zone. Good boots with cushion and a walking stick will help, but still expect a solid dose of foot pounding before reaching your final destination. While tiring, the geology is interesting—at the low- and mid-tide zone, layers of black siltstone and orange sandstone jut up. Dating back to the Cretaceous age, about 100 million years ago, these rocks are an ancient seabed uplifted to the surface, providing foothold and perches on the beach for life today. Keep an eye out for layers of rock with fossilized shell fragments and the odd bit of coal.

About an hour west of Wolftrack Beach is Christensen Point, a prominent knuckle of land marked by a bright buoy hanging from a pair of spruce trees. The trees lean together towards the ocean and a long-gone nurse log has left a cylindrical window in their conjoined roots. The route ahead is a straight stretch of beach, completely void of coves or curving headlands. Once at Christensen Point you are just over 3 km (1.86 mi) from Laura Creek—the home stretch!

LAURA CREEK CAMPSITE

THE LAURA CREEK CAMPSITE is not actually located at its name-sake creek, but about 200 m (650 ft) west of it. Cross the creek (careful of slippery rocks) and continue along the beach until you see buoys and the BC Parks sign. The campsite is tucked in the shelter of the forest just off the rocky beach. The towering conifers and dense undergrowth of salal offer a protective canopy and windbreak. There is a shelter with a cooking area and benches. Four tent pads are connected by dirt pathways, and the salal provides adequate privacy between the sites. A food locker is nearby, but located uncomfortably close to one of the tent pads. An outhouse is set to the back of the campsite, furthest from the ocean. Water access is (perhaps obviously) from Laura Creek.

While not the most picturesque campsite, Laura Creek is located at a convenient break point for tired hikers. A good way to stretch the weary legs—and possibly take an ocean swim—is to wander west from the campsite along the 1-km (0.6-mi) beach. Here, at mid- to low-tide, there is soft sand, smooth rocks, and a little creek running out to the ocean. Back at camp, at the edge of the forest, there is plenty of driftwood to sit against. At high tide, the waves come close. The rest feels more than great, and you've certainly earned it at this point. Use caution when doing dishes in the tide here, as the rocks are slippery with green seaweed. The next morning, you'll likely be woken by chuckling ravens and eagles calling from the trees above and encouraging you onwards.

A! Camping space can be an issue at Laura Creek. With only four tent pads and limited beach camping (due to a narrow beach and cobblestones) it is best to arrive early to secure a site. Large groups should not camp here as they would leave little camping space for others. If the campground is full, there may be a small sandbar suitable for camping next to the mouth of Laura Creek. But pay attention to high tides and rising river levels during heavy rains. If the Laura Creek campsite is full when you arrive, you might be forced to either press on, or set up in an uncomfortable location. Additional shelter or an expansion of the Laura Creek campsite is being considered by BC Parks. As the North Coast Trail gets busier, it may even be necessary to implement a reservation system here.

TRAIL SECTION 5

LAURA CREEK TO NISSEN BIGHT
Map 5 — 36.1–43.1 km (22.4–26.8 mi)

A LOVELY INLAND SECTION full of creeks, streams, a boggy plateau, and Laughing Loon Lake. Nissen Bight provides the loveliest reward to finish the day.

HIKING TIME: 3–5 hours
DISTANCE: 7 km (around 4.3 mi)
DIFFICULTY: Moderate
TERRAIN: Inland forest ecosystem. A moist environment with several creek crossings. Moderate elevation gain to upland bog plateau. Douglas fir forest near Nissen Bight.
HIGHLIGHTS: Several beautiful creek beds, mossy terrain, Laughing Loon Lake, and Nissen Bight.

SPECIAL CONSIDERATIONS

 Nissen Bight marks the official beginning (or end) of the North Coast Trail

---

WHILE THE WHOLE TRAIL is contained within the Cape Scott Provincial Park boundaries, in many people's minds, Nissen Bight is the dividing line between the official North Coast Trail and the Cape Scott side of the park.

BREAK CAMP FROM LAURA Creek at a respectable hour and you can arrive at Nissen Bight with time to spare. The 7-km (4.3-mi) trek should take 3–5 hours of steady going. You'll revisit the upland bog ecosystem you experienced near Shushartie Bay,

Beach rock west of Laura Creek. *Photo: Andrew Bruce Lau*

but the terrain on this side is noticeably easier. By this stage in the trail you should have found your hiking legs. As your fitness improves, the natural rewards are easier to spot beneath the weight of your bag. Regardless of your fitness, Nissen Bight is a definite highlight.

Aside from a small beach section immediately west of Laura Creek, this section is entirely inland. Expect some climbing and elevation gain as the trail travels up towards the inland plateau and skirts the Nahwitti Cone. The trail from Laura Creek to Nissen Bight mostly follows the old settlers' trail. Along the way you can see old bridges and graded sections of trail built to accommodate wagon traffic. Water access is not an issue along this section—the environment is moist and there are several creek crossings. Keep your eyes open to spot several large old-growth cedars around Dakota Creek. After passing Laughing Loon Lake (the only lake along the trail), you will begin the descent down to Nissen Bight, which is sandy, calm, and a true reward.

THE BEACH WEST OF Laura Creek makes for a beautiful and mellow start to this section. The upper beach is made of cobblestones and driftwood but low tide reveals a sandy plain. Interesting humps of rock protrude from the sand or lie in rubbly heaps amongst the waves. At the end of the beach, about 1 km (around 0.6 mi) from the campsite, a small but reliable creek provides good water access.

Just after the creek, head into the forest and follow a beautiful trail leading steadily upwards. A long staircase ducks under a fallen cedar, taking you deeper inland and higher into the woods. The trail skirts around the Nahwitti Cone and several rocky headlands. The trail misses the Cone's summit (186 m or around 610 ft), but don't be shy of a little elevation gain as you hike upwards through a muddy trail and deeper into the forest towards a minor upland plateau. The stubby, rough vegetation is reminiscent of the inland section from Shushartie Bay, but several pretty creek crossings make for a more scenic trail than you experienced earlier.

This is a lush environment teaming with life: beds of moss, clusters of mushrooms, lichens, ferns, huckleberry, salal, ancient cedars, and new saplings nursing on the shoulders of their ancestors. There are brief sections of upland bog ecosystem. While the terrain is not as taxing as what lies to the east, mud, twisted roots, and steep climbs provide regular reminders that you are working for this reward. After crossing Dakota Creek (unmarked but described

Sturdy construction makes the forest trail relatively easy.

83

Fresh living water along the forest trail between Laura Creek and Nissen Bight. *Photo: Andrew Bruce Lau*

below), keep an eye out for more signs of the corduroy road—a lingering symbol of the settlers' stamina and isolation, and a humbling reminder of the relative ease of your few days of modern-equipped adventure.

WATER, WATER, EVERYWHERE

AS THE TRAIL SKIRTS around the slopes of the Nahwitti Cone, it passes through a natural water catchment area. The terrain is moist and, at times, quite boggy. Several creeks and streams weave through the landscape. This is lucky news for thirsty hikers, who can fill their bottles at these four water crossings:

1. Small stream, 2 km (around 1.2 mi) from Laura Creek. Crossing is via a boardwalk bridge.

2. Dakota Creek, at kilometre 39 (mile 24). A felled tree creates a sturdy bridge for hikers and a whimsical rooftop decorates the

remaining stump. The water flow is good, but the height of the bridge makes access somewhat awkward.

3. Less than 30 minutes from Dakota Creek (or 2 hours from Laura Creek) a tributary feeding into Dakota Creek provides excellent water access. The water is clear, the current is swift, and access is easy. No bridge runs across this creek and blue flagging tape has been added to deter using the slippery log to cross, but this creek can be crossed easily by stepping along larger pebbles in the shallower section. The idyllic setting is worthy of at least a few minutes to enjoy the sound of the running water, the mossy river rock, and lush vegetation.

4. There is a fourth stream crossing via a small boardwalk, right after the tributary described above. This water source is also excellent.

FROM THIS FINAL CREEK, another hill climb takes you up to a brief plateau (76 m or around 249 ft elevation) and Laughing Loon Lake. Stretching about 400 m (around 1,312 ft), the lake creates a beautiful, open setting. Reliable boardwalk surrounds the lake, making a good spot for reflection or rest. The surrounding vegetation is a blend of stunted cedar and ponderosa pine, hemlock, lichen moss, grasses, and reeds. Early in the season, the surrounding shore

Upland bog descending to Nissen Bight. *Photo: Andrew Bruce Lau*

is marshy and damp. Later, a hodge-podge of animal tracks can be found in the cracked and drying mud—an indication that this place gets more traffic than the stillness implies. The lake can be stagnant in the summer and, with easy water access elsewhere on this route, it is best for admiring, not drinking from.

From Laughing Loon Lake, it is less than 3 km (1.86 mi) or around 45 minutes of fairly easy hiking to Nissen Bight. The trail continues west along the upland plateau for a few hundred metres, followed by a gradual descent into the forest, heading northwest to the ocean. As you leave the plateau, most of the trail construction gives way to dirt path with several scrambles over logs and roots. There are several muddy sections, made wider in places by hikers trying to avoid the muck.

A log crossing over a minor water source means that you are less than 20 minutes from Nissen Bight. The trail rounds a bend and begins a short but steep descent down the hillside. Here, the ecosystem changes dramatically. Open, scrubby woodland becomes lush rainforest, thick with salal, ferns, and old-growth forest. You can hear the waves crashing below and the atmosphere takes on the cool dampness of ocean air. You know you are close! Over 40 stairs take you the final way down to sea level.

 Just before reaching the beach, you come to the trailhead buoy marking the official beginning (or end) of the North Coast Trail. A buoy strung up on a tree directs hikers to either the freshwater source, or to the North Coast Trail (from where you've come). Head straight to go directly out to the beach, which by now, is likely calling your name. If you need water, collect it here to save backtracking later.

NISSEN BIGHT

BEFORE THE NORTH COAST Trail was built, Nissen Bight offered the most northern beach camping of Cape Scott Provincial Park. Now, it is the gateway to the North Coast Trail. From Nissen Bight, it is just 15 km (around 9.3 mi) to the San Josef/ Cape Scott trailhead or 5.8 km (around 3.6 mi) to Nels Bight. Whatever your destination, be sure to take a rest at Nissen Bight and savour this fantastic beach. If time and weather are on your side, stay longer. While not as popular as Nels Bight, there is something attractive about Nissen Bight's smaller size and protected bay. A shorter, narrower cousin to Shuttleworth Bight, Nissen Bight also offers expansive views, perfect sunsets,

WATER AT NISSEN BIGHT

The only water access is at the east side of the bight. If you have camped at the west side of the bight near the trail sign, this means a 900-m (2,952-ft) beach walk—about 20 minutes each way. If you are arriving from the direction of Laura Creek and are tired, it makes sense to collect water as soon as you arrive to avoid backtracking from your campsite. From the buoy in the forest, a short trail leads you to a small reservoir (fed by a stream connected to Laughing Loon Lake). At low tide, you can access the reservoir by beach if you prefer. The water is plentiful and reliable. Respect others and do not bathe or wash dishes in this slow-moving pool. If you are coming from the direction of the Cape Scott trailhead or Nels, you may want to consider collecting water from a stream about 15 minutes south of Nissen. This will save you the 40-minute walk to the official, but "far east" Nissen Bight water source.

and great swimming. The sand is a welcome relief from difficult beach and forest hiking and you'll undoubtedly want to stay longer. Several ramshackle driftwood huts and windbreaks (or their remnants) are scattered along the length of the beach—all signs that others also consider this a place worth lingering at.

CAMPING IS POSSIBLE ALONG the length of Nissen Bight, but you will find the sandiest areas from mid- to west beach. Outhouses, the BC Parks sign, and a map are also located on the west side, just within the forest. Water access is nearly a kilometre away at the east side of the beach (see page 87). There are food lockers at both sides of the beach—one by the BC Parks sign at the west end, and the other by the North Coast Trail trailhead on the east end.

From the west side of Nissen Bight, you can also access Fisherman Bay. Its steep rocky shores are not great for camping, but the pretty little cove is worth visiting. Take a very short forest path from the outhouse to the bay, or you can view it from the black rock outcropping at the edge of the beach (these rocks also have tide pools and beautiful small shells). Fisherman Bay was prominent in the lives of the settlers (see page 155). To add further protection to the bay than provided by nature, an old ship was sunk to create a breakwater. Harsh winter storms pummeled it apart and remnants of it can still be seen when the tide is low. Today, boats still use Fisherman Bay as a sheltered mooring area.

After several nights on the North Coast, a night at Nissen Bight is icing on the cake. Replace your urban walls with the limits of the horizon, tidal lines, and forest. Dig your toes into the sand and don't be in a rush to leave just yet.

Nissen Bight, looking east. *Photo: Andrew Bruce Lau*

TRAIL SECTION 6

NISSEN BIGHT TO NELS BIGHT
*Map 5 — 43.1–44.8 km (26.8–28 mi) to the junction;
0–3.8 km (0–2.2 mi) junction to Nels Bight*

HIKE THROUGH QUIET FOREST trails, beautiful meadows, and the original Cape Scott settlement.

HIKING TIME: 2 hours
DISTANCE: 5.8 km (3.6 mi)
DIFFICULTY: Easy
TERRAIN: Forest hiking, open meadows, tidal flats, and the estuary of Hansen Lagoon.
HIGHLIGHTS: Historic remains from the Cape Scott settlement, meadows, and Nels Bight.

SPECIAL CONSIDERATIONS

None

WITH THE GIFT OF blissfully easy hiking, there is little excuse not to slow down and take in the sights and natural wonders along this section. It's not just nature you will find here—the trail from Nissen Bight to Nels Bight provides a window into one of the most historically significant areas of the park. A variety of motives and aspirations have drawn people here for centuries. The region was a hub of activity for First Nations communities and Danish settlers. The Cape Scott settlement (1897–1918) was centered around the area from Nels/Nissen junction to the fertile land around Hansen Lagoon. The Danish settlers inhabited this area for a few decades, but Kwakwaka'wakw First Nations have a history here that dates back thousands of years. The

A cool coastal morning at Nels Bight. *Photo: Steve Fines*

area's importance is underlined by its place as a focal point in many of their legends. Nels Bight itself was once known as T'sa̱'wa̱nx̱as or "winter place," and may have been a village of the G̱usgimukw (anglicized as Koskimo) people.

Today this area, including Cape Scott, is probably the most well known and well travelled in the park. Cape Scott is by no means a hiking highway, but expect to cross paths with more than a few people in the summer. From the Nissen/Nels junction, getting to the west arm of the park is an out-and-back hike so you can take in the scenery both on your arrival and your departure.

History, nature, and easy hiking aside, the journey is worth it for beautiful Nels Bight alone. The area has expansive sand beaches, ocean air, and beautiful sunsets—you couldn't ask for much more.

IT TAKES APPROXIMATELY 2 hours to get from Nissen Bight to Nels Bight. From Nissen Bight, a trail at the west side of the beach (near the outhouses and BC Parks sign) leads into the forest and south. The terrain is mostly flat, although there is a gradual incline as you move away from sea level. In the days of the Cape Scott settlement, this was known by the school children as Lard Hill, perhaps referring to the slippery-as-lard mud that accumulates with the rain. But with no roots to scramble up and over, the hiking is fast and easy. The straight trails follow roads established by the settlers more than a century ago, making them among the easiest in the park. Within 30 minutes you should reach the junction.

NELS/NISSEN JUNCTION

AROUND 2 KM (1.2 mi) south of Nissen Bight (44.8 km or 27.8 mi from the Shushartie Bay trailhead), you reach a T-shaped junction in the trail. Continuing straight (or southbound) from the junction will take you to the San Josef/Cape Scott parking lot and trailhead (13.1 km or around 8.1 mi and about 4.5 hours). To reach Cape Scott and the west arm of the park, go right at the junction. Nels Bight is just 3.8 km (around 2.4 mi) or about 1.5 hours away, and Experiment Bight, Guise Bay, and the Cape Scott lighthouse are further ahead.

ON YOUR WAY TO Nels Bight, the trail continues along the historic road and through a major part of the original Cape Scott settlement. The trail passes the old school/community hall, the post office, and a dozen or so former homestead sites. While nature has hidden many of these signs, there are still many visible remnants of the settlers' past: farm implements, foundations, old stoves and pipes, gravestones, and even a tractor. Left behind and now out of place in the rainforest, these artifacts linger as a fading monument to the efforts of the people who

Old dikes at Hansen Lagoon meadows.

tried to establish a life here. One of the most resilient was Alfred Spencer, the longest-lasting European settler of this area who remained at Cape Scott until 1956. As you continue through the forest, look for the sign marking Spencer's old farm.

About 1,200 m (3,937 ft) from the Nels/Nissen junction, you reach Hansen Lagoon meadows. A sign provides a map and a good history of the area. Looking at the flat, open fields rimmed with low-lying hills, one can understand how the seed of an idea grew in the mind of Rasmus Hansen and his fellow settlers. In 1896, they wrote to the Minister of Immigration to request permission to farm this region. They received his approval and what appear as linear creeks today are actually the remains of ditches dug by settlers in their attempts to drain the boggy meadows. The settlers also made two attempts at diking the lagoon to keep the tide out and, for a brief time, the meadows grew hay and crops. Now, only occasional fence posts stand stubbornly upright, delineating the old fields but keeping nothing in or out. See page 155 for more information on the history of the area.

PACIFIC FLYWAY

Hansen Lagoon is a major north-south travel route for migratory birds, whose route extends all the way from the Arctic Circle, down the Pacific Coast to Patagonia. Every year, migratory birds travel some or all of this distance, both in spring and in fall, following food sources, and travelling to breeding grounds and overwintering sites. These feathered endurance athletes include Canada geese, spotted sandpipers, great blue herons, sandhill cranes, trumpeter swans, semipalmated plovers, terns, and snipes.

From the sign at Hansen Lagoon meadows, a brief detour to the lagoon is possible if you continue straight (west). But note that this sub-trail may be overgrown and not obvious. If you can find it, expect to hike about 1 km until you reach the lagoon.

Wolf sighting in Hansen Lagoon meadows. *Photo: Cathy Denham*

Here, you may see the remains of the settlers' dike and a steam boiler from the old sawmill. The saltwater marsh and tidal mud flats of Hansen Lagoon stretches 5 km (around 3.1 mi) from tip to ocean outlet at Hansen Bay. The lagoon is a significant habitat for migratory birds, providing a stopover for tired wings looking for a place to rest and feed. Birders know this as part of the Pacific Flyway. It is a rich habitat—cutthroat trout are also found in these waters, and the area was popular with First Nations and European settlers for harvesting shells. In the mornings and evenings, wolves can often be seen at the meadows.

To reach Nels Bight from the sign at Hansen Lagoon meadows, take the main trail veering right (northwest). A small wooden bridge takes you across Hansen Creek. The trail continues west through the meadow to the top of Hansen Lagoon. At this point you are only 2 km (around 1.2 mi) away from Nels Bight. The trail returns to the forest and the hiking is flat and easy. Despite your anticipation to get to Nels Bight, slow down. Enjoy the environment and keep an eye out for

Tidal backwash at Nels Bight. *Photo: Steve Fines*

amphibians underfoot and the little side trails that offer views of the lagoon.

NELS BIGHT

NELS BIGHT IS THE most popular beach in the Cape Scott Provincial Park, and not without reason. It can be reached within a day from the San Josef/Cape Scott trailhead (a distance of 17 km or around 10.6 mi), making it an accessible weekend destination. North Coast Trail hikers are in the minority here—most visitors are weekenders coming to enjoy the west side of the park. Despite this popularity, you needn't feel crowded.

The beach at Nels Bight is expansive, stretching over 2 km (1.2 mi) long and, when the tide is out, over 200 m (around 650 ft) wide. Nels Bight is the most common launch pad for day trips to the Cape Scott lighthouse and surrounding area, but it is also a

Sunset at Nels Bight.

worthwhile destination itself. The beach is stunning—sandy and flat, it's a westward-facing Pacific paradise that offers the best sunsets on the trail, endlessly rolling waves, and wide-open skies.

Nels Bight is bound by Frederiksen Point to the east and, to the west, a rocky bluff that hides the cape. In good weather, it is heaven on earth but when wild coastal storms rage, it bears the brunt of the harsh winds.

Camping is in vast supply at Nels Bight—anywhere above the high tide zone on the beach is perfect. If the weather looks moody, find an area behind the large driftwood logs for a natural windbreak and potential place to string a tarp. At the east side of the beach, several cleared spaces in the forest provide additional shelter. For convenience and safety, food lockers and pit toilets are distributed along the beach at three locations: on the west side, near the water source, between the river and the trailhead, and at the northeast end of the beach.

The primary water access is from a creek at the west end of the beach. The water is full of tannins, giving it a brown hue even when filtered. Pre-filter it if possible (through a t-shirt, coffee filter, or whatever is convenient) to save the life of your water filter. It is a good idea to clean your filter after several pulls from here. Another stream feeds out onto the beach at the north end of the beach.

A new ranger station (built in 2014) in the middle of the bight is occupied by Park Facility Operators from June to September, and at various times through the year for management purposes. At other times, the cabin will be left unlocked and may be used as an emergency shelter (it is furnished with a wood stove for warmth and to dry gear). However, visitors must be prepared to camp at any time and should not rely on the availability of the facility. If you use this shelter, please leave it as you found it, if not better.

New ranger cabin at Nels Bight. *Photo: David Wall*

TRAIL SECTION 7

NELS BIGHT TO CAPE SCOTT: GUISE BAY, EXPERIMENT BIGHT AND THE LIGHTHOUSE
Map 6 — 3.8–10.4 km (2.4–6.5 mi)

ENTER A STUNNING LANDSCAPE — in every windswept corner, legend and overgrown history lingers.

HIKING TIME: 2.5 hours one way

DISTANCE: 6.6 km (around 4.1 mi) one way

DIFFICULTY: Easy/Moderate

TERRAIN: Beaches, sand dunes, and forest trail.

HIGHLIGHTS: The Sand Neck (dunes, meadows, and wild strawberries), Guise Bay and Experiment Bight, the Cape Scott lighthouse, First Nations and European history.

	SPECIAL CONSIDERATIONS
	Limited drinking water. Pack it in.
	Unofficial camping opportunity at Experiment Bight with limited facilities (no outhouses or food lockers). Be sure to cache food properly at both Guise and Experiment beaches. Wolves and bears are common here.

CAPE SCOTT IS THE most well-known area of the park. Only 23.2 km (14.4 mi) from the San Josef/Cape Scott trailhead, it is a popular destination for a weekend backpacking trip. But despite this relative accessibility, the cape remains wild. It is known for its rich heritage and cultural significance and this is rivalled only by its stunning physical landscape. Beautiful coastal vistas are available and you can find rocky headlands, ocean views,

Bowen's Beach (just west of Nels Bight).

tranquil forests, sandy beaches, dunes, and grassland meadows. A sense of resilience and stubborn fortitude permeates the land. From a bird's-eye view, the cape stretches out to the Pacific as if to join the Scott Islands or, perhaps more in line with its rugged independence, take to the open ocean alone.

The cape is a must-see, so make sure to save time in your hiking itinerary for the day trip. This side of the park features some of the best beaches alongside the unique sand dunes and historic sites. At the furthest point of it all is the Cape Scott lighthouse, located on the northern tip of the cape beyond the park boundary on Department of National Defence land. While this area is most popular as a day hike from Nels Bight, camping is possible at Guise Bay and Experiment Bight.

USING NELS BIGHT AS a base camp, the hike to the Cape Scott lighthouse and surrounding area can be explored in a day, with time to spare. Budget 5 hours for a return hike and more if you plan to picnic and relax. The trail to Cape Scott (including the lighthouse, Guise Bay, and Experiment Bight) begins in the forest at the west side of Nels Bight beside the ranger station. In March 2012, heavy rains caused a landslide on the trail between Nels Bight and Experiment Bight. The trail has been repaired but use caution when crossing this section of trail during high wind and rain.

The forest trail avoids impassable rocky headlands and, after about 1,200 m (around 4,000 ft), emerges at the first beach, known as Bowen's Beach after a homesteader who built his cabin here. Walk along the white sand until buoys guide you back into the forest. From here, the trail follows some of the old corduroy road, travelling southwest until arriving at the grassy sand dunes of Guise Bay about 90 minutes later.

The trail takes you to the east side of Guise Bay. This south-facing, sheltered cove offers a wide sand beach, turquoise waters and is perhaps one of the most beautiful beaches in the park. You can picnic here, swim in the cold ocean water, or even camp on the beach with few or no neighbours. There is a food locker, and water access is from a small stream at the southeast side of the bay (marked by floats). On the east side of Guise Bay, just up from the beach, is a path leading to an outhouse and the remnants of World War II outpost buildings.

The sand neck separating Experiment Bight and Guise Bay is one of the most interesting features of this area. This thin tendon of land is the only thing connecting the knobby finger of the cape to Vancouver Island. The First Nations called this place Apdzeges, meaning "against each other." When standing at a high vantage point on the windswept dunes and grass, you can see why. Ocean waves from the two beaches come in from either direction, as if in opposition. Or perhaps they are working together for a common goal. Either way, the tides will eventually absorb the land and the cape will become an island.

Around 1910, a settler named Nels P. Jensen built a series of fences here to contain his livestock. The driftwood posts you

can spot half-buried or crooked in these dunes are another reminder of the settlers' attempts to tame this sea-swept terrain.
Jensen's grave is in the grass on the western side of these dunes.

On the north side of the sand neck is Experiment Bight—a sandy, north-facing sister-beach to Guise Bay. Access to Experiment
Bight is via a trail from the west side of Guise Bay. Camping is
possible here but there are no outhouses or food lockers so be
sure to practise good backcountry etiquette with your human
waste (or use the toilets at Guise Bay) and bring your own rope
to create a bear-proof food locker. Water is available from a seasonal stream mid-beach at Experiment Bight.

Experiment Bight, known as Gwigwakawalis to the Kwak-
wa̱ka̱'wakw, was a seasonal village and is referenced frequently
in local legend and stories. It is said that you can see the footprint
of the Transformer K'aniki'lakw pushed into the rocks (most
Northwest Coast First Nations groups believe that the state of

Guise Bay

Nels P. Jensen's misspelled gravestone at Guise Bay.
Photo: Dave Trebett

things in the present was brought from myth into being by the Transformer). Among other feats, legend has it that K'aniki'lakw was able to step to Triangle Island from here in a single stride.

From Guise Bay, the trail climbs uphill, following a World War II-era plank road used to access a military radar station, and now home to the lighthouse. About 2.5 hours and 6.6 km (around 4.1 mi) from Nels Bight, you reach the red and white buildings of the lighthouse.

The Cape Scott lighthouse was built in 1960. Its buildings and grounds are kept in immaculate condition and staffed by Coast Guard lightkeepers, currently Harvey and Todd. This civilized destination point is definitely an attraction, and not just for the junk food that the keepers often have for sale. The

Experiment Bight. *Photo: Dave Trebett*

lighthouse can be climbed for a wide-open view of the Pacific Ocean, and the manicured lawns and summer sunshine attract picnickers and tired backpackers, who nap on the grass or find ways to ingest peanut butter from various states of recline. While there used to be a trail to the tip of the cape, deterioration of the suspension bridges and boardwalk led to the decommissioning of the trail.

Opposite, top: The Cape Scott lighthouse.
Opposite, bottom: Arriving at the lighthouse.

TRAIL SECTION 8

NELS BIGHT TO THE SAN JOSEF/CAPE SCOTT TRAILHEAD, INCLUDING ERIC LAKE AND FISHERMAN RIVER CAMPSITES
Maps 6 and 7 — 3.8–0 km (2.4–0 mi) to the junction, 44.8–57.6 km (27.8–35.8 mi)

THIS ROUTE IS THE core artery in and out of the park, providing access to Cape Scott lighthouse, beautiful beaches, and the gateway to the North Coast Trail.

HIKING TIME: 6–7.5 hours

DISTANCE: 16.8 km (10.4 mi)

DIFFICULTY: Moderate due to the distance

TERRAIN: Forest hiking through lush trails, boardwalk, and muddy sections. A relatively flat trail with minor undulations.

HIGHLIGHTS: Beautiful rainforest, Eric Lake, giant Sitka spruce and other old-growth trees. First Nations history and signs of European settlement including old telegraph lines and the corduroy road.

	SPECIAL CONSIDERATIONS
☁	Weather conditions will affect the difficulty and time required to complete this route.
💧	Plentiful water sources. Fisherman River is the best source. Eric Lake offers water access, as do several small creeks further south.
🚌	Transportation logistics at trailhead.
☆	Trailhead

PRIOR TO THE DEVELOPMENT of the North Coast Trail, the section from the San Josef/Cape Scott trailhead to Nels Bight was the only defined Cape Scott trail. Today, this route remains a core artery of the park, providing access to Cape Scott lighthouse and beautiful beaches. But this section now also provides entry or exit to the North Coast Trail and options for hikers seeking longer, or more remote wilderness adventures.

The terrain along this section is relatively flat and easy. With decent fitness and an average pace, it is possible to hike from Nels Bight to the trailhead in a single day. However, the 17 km (around 10.6 mi) distance can make this a challenging day hike, particularly in wet conditions. Cape Scott's knee-deep, slippery mud is almost legendary. No child or pet has been lost to the thick slop, but many a boot and hiking pole has! Today, extensive stretches of flat boardwalk guide you over the worst sections, but don't expect to get away unscathed. Boardwalk can be extremely slippery when wet; use caution and take it slow. If you have them, put your gaiters on for this section.

Keep weather conditions in mind when planning your hike, especially if you plan to catch the early afternoon shuttle bus. Allow plenty of time for unforeseen delays. An obvious highlight is the historic remains of the Cape Scott settlement, (see page 167 historic map for an index of these sites of interest). There are some interpretive signs, but keep your eyes out for unmarked bridle trails that lead to some of these old landmarks.

Evidence of old telegraph lines.

107

Rays through trees on the Cape Scott trail. *Photo: Steve Fines*

NELS BIGHT (INCLUDING FISHERMAN RIVER CAMPSITE) TO ERIC LAKE

IT IS 13.7 KM (around 8.5 mi) from Nels Bight to the Eric Lake campsite. Budget 5–6 hours to cover this ground. The route is flat but can be muddy and wet. The first few kilometres retrace your steps from the hike in—you'll return through the Hansen Lagoon meadows. As you near the Nels/Nissen junction and the original Cape Scott settlement area, the forest thins and several side trails lead to remnants of the homesteads and farms that once stood here.

At the junction, turn right, heading south towards the trail-head and Eric Lake (left would take you north to Nissen Bight). From here, it is another 3.2 km (around 2 mi) to Fisherman River. Much of the surrounding environment is open forest and swampy meadows. The way is straight and flat. Until the trail-head, you will be walking along extensive sections of boardwalk as well as remnants of the old settlers' road.

Fisherman River provides an excellent water source and a small, rarely used camping area with two tent pads and an outhouse. A log bridge provides crossing over the river. The area is peaceful and makes a great stop to break and refill water bottles. From here, it is just 6.7 km (around 4.2 mi) to the Eric Lake campsite, or 9.6 km (around 6 mi or about 3 hours) to the San Josef/Cape Scott trailhead.

Rustic sign for Fisherman River. *Photo: Steve Fines*

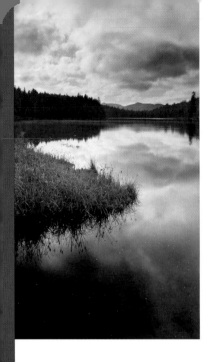

Eric Lake. *Photo: Steve Fines*

From Fisherman River, the environment becomes much more forested, with a few more challenging undulations, roots, and minor scrambles. The trail continues south and runs parallel to Saint Mary Creek. The creek bed creates flat, easy hiking through lush undergrowth and massive trees. Spot the old telegraph lines and the original corduroy road in this section. Keep an eye out for a giant Sitka spruce over 7 m (around 23 ft) in circumference about 20 minutes north of Eric Lake. Located on the east side of the trail, it is almost impossible to miss. See map for location.

Through the trees you will glimpse a large body of water, which tells you that you're nearing Eric Lake. The campsite is located about 600 m (1,969 ft) from the top of the lake, just inside the forest. You've officially arrived when you pass the outhouses along the boardwalk. Because of its size and proximity to the San Josef/Cape Scott trailhead, Eric Lake is a common campsite for large groups, families, and late hikers. There are 11 tent pads within the forest and it's a tranquil place, but for the urgent hum of thirsty mosquitoes. Prepare with long-sleeved clothing and bug repellent. Food lockers are provided and there is water access from Eric Lake or the small creek running through the campsite. As with any campsite (but especially here given its high use), please stay on the boardwalk areas to avoid damage to the plant life. Also take care to avoid contaminating the lake and creek with any soap or food waste.

ERIC LAKE TO THE SAN JOSEF/CAPE SCOTT TRAILHEAD

IT IS ONLY 3 km (1.9 mi) or 1.5–2 hours of hiking from the Eric Lake campsite to the trailhead. A true rainforest, the trail has several small creeks and rivulets, and the abundant plant life (ferns, lilies, and mosses) drips with moisture. The terrain is generally flat and boardwalk traverses the wettest sections, but expect to negotiate the odd root system and mud hole. If the boardwalk is wet, take special care.

Depending on your state of mind and body, you might be hungry for the taste of civilization, quietly dreading the return to the real world, or both. As you near the park's western trailhead, a junction in the trail marks a 2.5 km (1.6 mi) diversion to San Josef Bay. Continue straight if you are heading back to civilization—the trailhead is only 700 m (2,297 ft) away. The last section is easy walking along graded gravel trail. No more scrambles or boggy sections to contend with!

San Josef/Cape Scott trailhead and parking lot. *Photo: Andrew Bruce Lau*

View of the trailhead and parking lot.

A gravel parking lot greets you at the San Josef/Cape Scott trailhead and, in high summer, there will likely be a small army of cars waiting for their outdoorsy owners to return from walkabout. This trailhead is popular with both day-trippers and multi-day backpackers.

There are two outhouses, an information board, a fee payment station, a large shelter with covered picnic tables, and seasonally staffed ranger yurt at the trailhead. There are no commercial operations—you are still 64 km (around 40 mi) from Port Hardy. Water is available from a stream near the yurt.

Do not leave your bags unattended here. Black bears are common and have become bold foragers.

TRAIL SECTION 9

SAN JOSEF/CAPE SCOTT TRAILHEAD TO SAN JOSEF BAY
Map 8 — 0–2.5 km (0–1.6 mi)

THIS SHORT PATH TO idyllic San Josef Bay is one of the easiest ways to reach heaven on Earth.

HIKING TIME: 45 minutes one way

DISTANCE: 2.5 km (1.6 mi)

DIFFICULTY: Easy

TERRAIN: Forest hiking that descends through beautiful old-growth forest and the San Josef River valley. This trail is wheelchair accessible.

HIGHLIGHTS: Old-growth cedar, historic sites, and interpretive signs of the European settlement, sea stacks.

	SPECIAL CONSIDERATIONS
☆	Trailhead
⬥	No water at the first beach. Pack it in or access water at the second beach.
⌐	Carry tide tables if you plan on camping or visiting the second beach. There is an alternate inland route to access the second beach. This route is very rough and steep. Be aware of high tides and use the beach if possible.

If you have the time, visit San Josef Bay. If you don't have the time, make the time. San Josef Bay is one of Cape Scott Provincial Park's jewels and the beach is one of the best in the park. The trail is the easiest and most accessible—perfect for families

The three sisters on the San Josef Bay trail.

☆ or weary hikers. Take the Cape Scott trail from the San Josef/Cape Scott trailhead parking lot. About 0.75 km (around 0.5 mi) from the trailhead, you reach the turn-off to San Josef Bay (to the right the trail continues north to Eric Lake and the Cape Scott trail). To reach San Josef Bay, stay left. The trail gently descends through beautiful old-growth cedar forest. There are some spectacular tree formations along the way and the trail is well maintained, graded, and covered with hard-pack gravel. It is wheelchair accessible and even manageable with a stroller.

There are interpretive signs along the way, documenting some of the history of this area. You will pass the rotting remains of Henry Ohlsen's home, store, and post office (inhabited from 1908–1944). As you near the bay, you'll enter a marshy area along the San Josef River and its estuary. The walk takes a total of around 45 minutes.

At San Josef Bay, soft sand greets you. To your left (east) is the estuary and to your right (west) are ocean-eroded sea stacks and caves carved in the rocky bluffs. These are definitely worth exploring and can be accessed at low tide.

San Josef Bay has two beaches divided by rocky bluffs. To get to the second beach, pass by the sea stacks and caves at low tide (this may not be possible during heavy storms). At high tide, you can take a steep inland trail marked with buoys, but use common sense and caution as this trail is rough and hazardous.

CAMPING

THERE IS EXCELLENT CAMPING at both of San Josef Bay's beaches. The first beach is more convenient, but lacks water. The second beach is approximately 1 km (0.6 mi) west of the first beach, and is a little more secluded and offers water. Both have an outhouse.

Water is only available from a creek at San Josef Bay's second beach. This beach can be accessed at low tide by going around the rocky bluffs, so ensure that you are aware of the tides and time your trip accordingly. The alternate inland route is rough and difficult.

San Josef Bay. *Photo: Andrew Bruce Lau*

TRAIL SECTION 10

SAN JOSEF BAY TO MOUNT ST. PATRICK, SEA OTTER COVE, AND LOWRIE BAY
Map 8 — 2.5–10 km (1.6–6.2 mi)

A TRULY RUGGED AND strenuous journey to the most isolated areas of the park.

HIKING TIME: 7 hours one way
DISTANCE: 7.5 km (4.7 mi) one way
DIFFICULTY: Very difficult
TERRAIN: Steep, mostly forest hiking. Can be slippery in wet conditions. Expect rough, unmaintained conditions and fallen trees.
HIGHLIGHTS: Summit of Mount St. Patrick.

	SPECIAL CONSIDERATIONS
☁	Weather conditions affect the difficulty and time required to complete this route.
⚠	Challenging terrain.
⛔	Impassible headland/high tide zone.

THIS IS AN OUT-AND-BACK trip. Do not attempt this trail unless you are an experienced and fit hiker—it is a tiring hike and precarious in places. The trail receives no regular maintenance and travellers are few and far between. Visit both the BC Parks website and hiking forums for awareness of current conditions. Carry a compass, topographical maps, and be prepared for a rough and overgrown wilderness route.

From San Josef Bay, walk to the far end of the second (western) beach. Here, you will find a forest trail that leads steeply up. Expect switchbacks and then a minor descent to a ravine. From here, the trail is uphill until you reach the summit of Mount St. Patrick (420 m or 1,378 ft). You will reach a sign telling you to stay on trail and a junction. Stay left to access the summit (the right trail leads to Sea Otter Cove and you will miss the great views). As you near the top, the trail follows a ridge and the forest begins to open up. It is less than 2 km (1.2 mi) from sea level to summit, but it is a tiring climb.

Mount St. Patrick is designated as a special feature zone for its wetlands and upland bog environment. The scrubby, stunted vegetation here is similar to that seen near the Shushartie Bay upland plateau. If the weather is clear, you can experience some beautiful panoramic views and see Sea Otter Cove in the distance. From the summit, take the steep descent down the west side of the mountain to Sea Otter Cove. If your destination is Lowrie Bay, go left at the sign (otherwise, return to San Josef Bay by turning right and retracing your steps). From here, the trail gets significantly rougher. If conditions are wet, the trail can also be quite slippery.

Sea Otter Cove is located 5.6 km (3.5 mi) from San Josef Bay. It will take about 5 hours to hike between the two, or 3 hours from the summit of Mount St. Patrick. At Sea Otter Cove, several streams converge, and you can access this fresh water by bushwhacking up the creek about 100 m (328 ft) to get above the tidal mixing. There is some beach at Sea Otter Cove, and the route around the head of the cove is passable only at mid to low tide. This route also involves two tidal creek crossings.

The trail from Sea Otter Cove to Lowrie Bay is another 2 km (around 1.2 mi) and should take about 2 hours. Floats mark the way. At Lowrie Bay, you'll find a picturesque, isolated beach with fresh water and high-tide beach camping. There is a pit toilet and a small hut that could sleep two people if necessary.

117

DID YOU KNOW?

There used to be a brothel at Sea Otter Cove run by one tough lady! In 1911, Pansy Mae Stuttard and her husband Rupert operated a "blind pig's inn," described as "a place for drink and girls" on Helen Island (Stuttard's Island to the locals) at the mouth of Sea Otter Cove. The inn was a popular stopover for fishermen. Well-liked by the settlers, Pansy was also a registered nurse and delivered one of the (well-known settlers) Rasmussen family's babies. She left Cape Scott after a few years, making her way through the Vancouver brothels, and ending up building a tavern in Point Roberts. Here, she amassed a small fortune selling whiskey out the back door to thirsty prohibition-bound Americans. In 1958, the 84-year-old Pansy made headlines as the "Pistol Packin' Mamma." Surrounded by her big game trophies she defended herself against two thieves who broke into her White Rock house, shooting at them with her 12-gauge shotgun (just one from an arsenal of loaded weapons in her collection). She suffered a blow to the head and wasn't found until four days later. A panicked neighbour called an ambulance, a hearse, and a priest. With the bill for the hearse kept as a souvenir, Pansy remarked on her plans to live until 100: "the Lord don't want me and the Devil won't take me." Aside from being a fragile and ornamental annual flower, pansy can mean sissy, feeble, and effeminate. Pansy Mae redefined this word as a compliment.

MAPS

MAP LEGEND

☆ Trailhead

▬▬▬ Trail

⬤ Kilometre trail marking

⚠ Campsite

⬥ Water source

⬥ No water

↥ Alternate inland route

⦿ Point of interest

⬒ Cable car

⊖ Impassable at high tide

🅿 Parking

⎯⎯ 500 ft contour intervals

┌╴╴╴ BC Parks outline

▭ Beach (all types: sand, pebble, cobblestone, etc.)

▦ Marsh

▨ Indian reserve

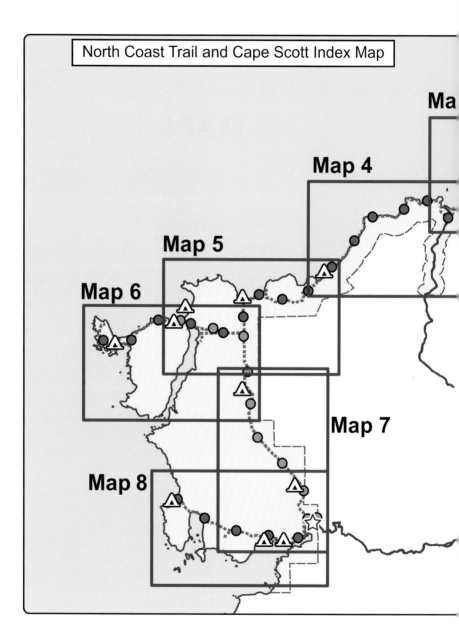

North Coast Trail and Cape Scott Index Map

Ma

Map 4

Map 5

Map 6

Map 7

Map 8

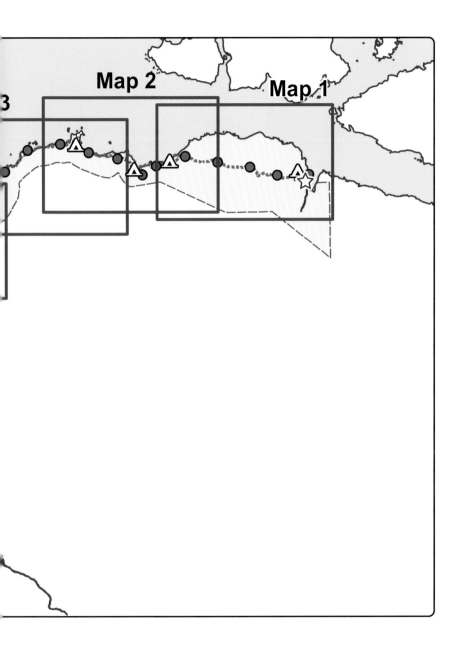

Map 1

Map 2

3

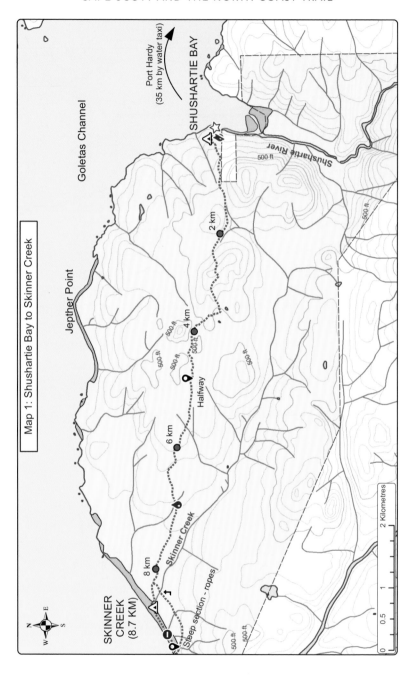

Map 1: Shushartie Bay to Skinner Creek

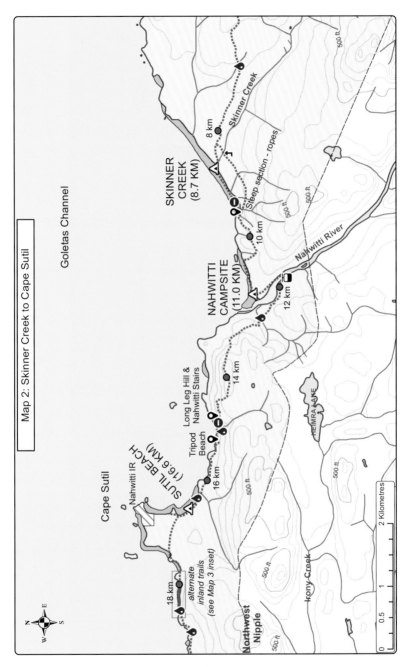

Map 2: Skinner Creek to Cape Sutil

Goletas Channel

Cape Sutil

Nahwitti IR

SUTIL BEACH
(16.6 KM)

alternate
inland trails
(see Map 3 inset)

18 km

Tripod
Beach

Long Leg Hill &
Nahwitti Stairs

16 km

14 km

NAHWITTI
CAMPSITE
(11.0 KM)

12 km

SKINNER
CREEK
(8.7 KM)

Steep section - ropes

10 km

8 km

Skinner Creek

Nahwitti River

HEMIRA LINE

Irony Creek

Northwest
Nipple

500 ft

500 ft

500 ft

500 ft

500 ft

500 ft

500 ft

0   0.5   1   2 Kilometres

N
W   E
S

123

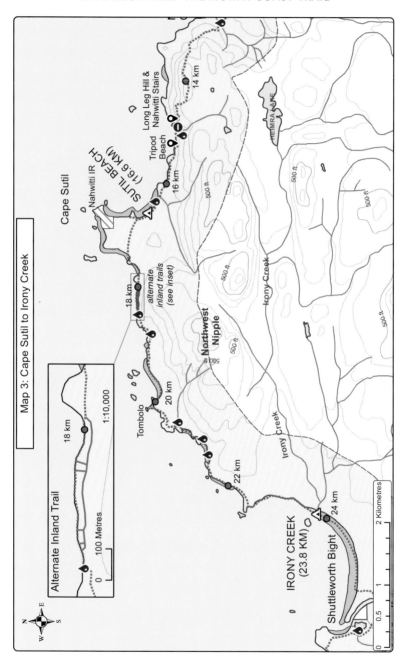

Map 3: Cape Sutil to Irony Creek

Cape Sutil

Nahwitti IR

SUTIL BEACH (16.6 KM)

Long Leg Hill & Nahwitti Stairs

Tripod Beach

14 km

16 km

CHEMRA LAKE

500 ft

500 ft

Irony Creek

18 km

alternate inland trails (see inset)

Northwest Nipple

500 ft

500 ft

500 ft

Tombolo

20 km

Irony Creek

22 km

IRONY CREEK (23.8 KM)

24 km

Shuttleworth Bight

Alternate Inland Trail

18 km

1:10,000

0   100 Metres

N
W   E
S

0   0.5   1   2 Kilometres

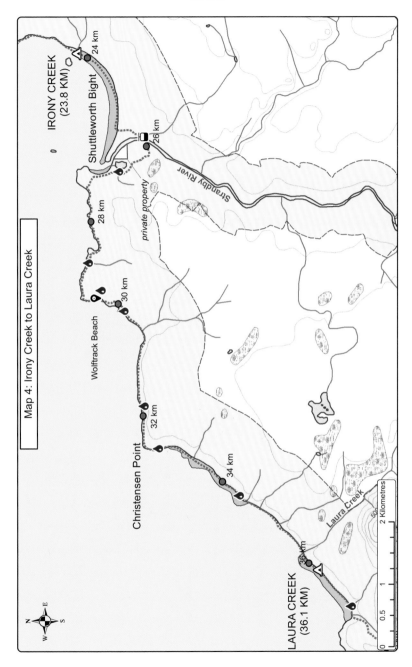

Map 4: Irony Creek to Laura Creek

IRONY CREEK
(23.8 KM)

Shuttleworth Bight

24 km

26 km

28 km

Strandby River

private property

Wolftrack Beach

30 km

Christensen Point

32 km

34 km

Laura Creek

36 km

LAURA CREEK
(36.1 KM)

N
W E
S

0   0.5   1   2 Kilometres

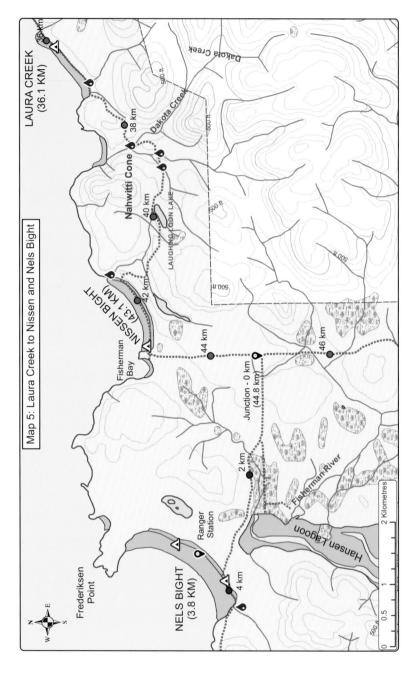

Map 5: Laura Creek to Nissen and Nels Bight

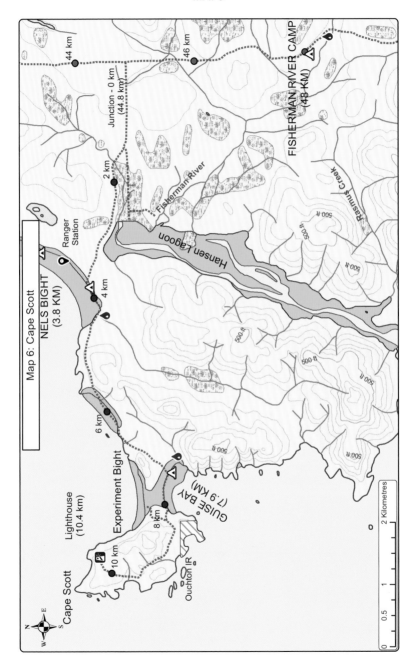

Map 6: Cape Scott

NELS BIGHT (3.8 KM)

Cape Scott

Lighthouse (10.4 km)

Experiment Bight

Ranger Station

GUISE BAY (7.9 KM)

Ouchton IR

Hansen Lagoon

Fisherman River

Rasmus Creek

FISHERMAN RIVER CAMP (48 KM)

Junction - 0 km (44.8 km)

44 km

46 km

2 km

4 km

6 km

8 km

10 km

500 ft

0   0.5   1   2 Kilometres

127

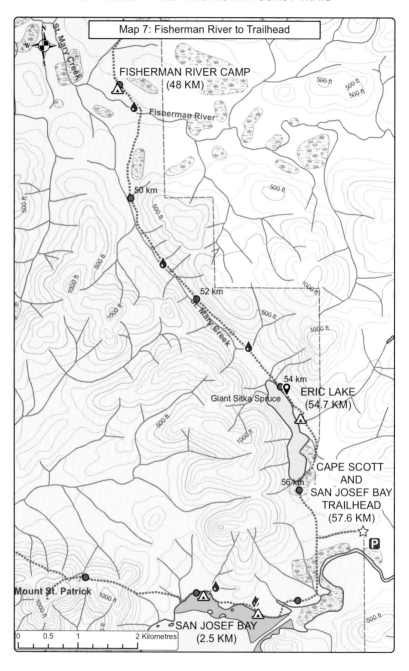

Map 7: Fisherman River to Trailhead

St. Mary Creek

FISHERMAN RIVER CAMP
(48 KM)

Fisherman River

50 km

52 km

St. Mary Creek

54 km

ERIC LAKE
(54.7 KM)

Giant Sitka Spruce

CAPE SCOTT
AND
SAN JOSEF BAY
TRAILHEAD
(57.6 KM)

56 km

Mount St. Patrick

0   0.5   1   2 Kilometres

SAN JOSEF BAY
(2.5 KM)

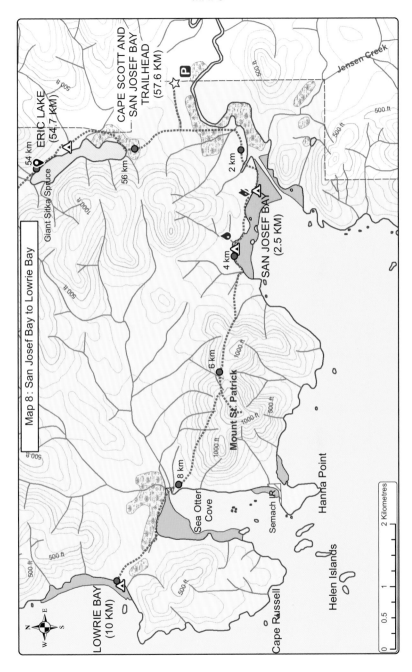

Map 8: San Josef Bay to Lowrie Bay

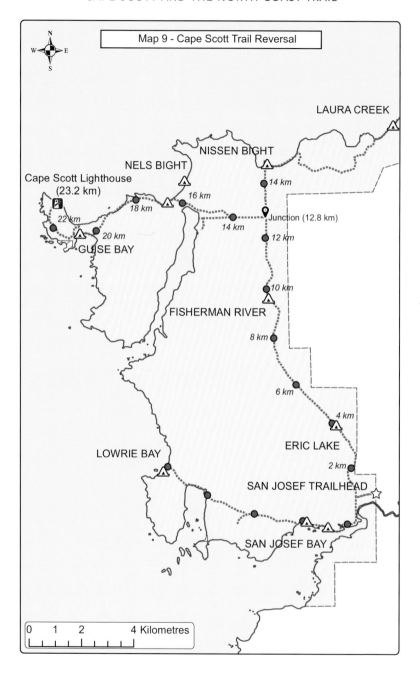

Map 9 - Cape Scott Trail Reversal

LAURA CREEK

NISSEN BIGHT

NELS BIGHT

Cape Scott Lighthouse
(23.2 km)

14 km

16 km

18 km

22 km

Junction (12.8 km)

14 km

12 km

20 km

GUISE BAY

10 km

FISHERMAN RIVER

8 km

6 km

4 km

LOWRIE BAY

ERIC LAKE

2 km

SAN JOSEF TRAILHEAD

SAN JOSEF BAY

0   1   2   4 Kilometres

ABBREVIATED TRAIL DESCRIPTIONS

TRAVELLING WEST TO EAST

THE TRAIL CHAPTERS IN this book are written from east to west (Shushartie Bay trailhead to the San Josef Bay/Cape Scott trailhead). Recognizing that not all will be hiking this direction, the following provides an at-a-glance summary of the trail sections from west to east (San Josef Bay/Cape Scott trailhead to Shushartie Bay trailhead). The in-depth trail descriptions will still be helpful.

SAN JOSEF/CAPE SCOTT TRAILHEAD TO ERIC LAKE
0–2.9 KM (0–1.8 MI)—MAP 9

San Josef/Cape Scott trailhead	DISTANCE: 2.9 km (1.8 mi)	Eric Lake
*Fee payment area	TIME: 1–1.5 hours	11 tent pads, food
Outhouse	DIFFICULTY: Easy	lockers, and outhouses

FROM THE GRAVEL PARKING lot, the trail immediately enters the rainforest. About 700 m (2,297 ft) from the trailhead, a junction leads to either San Josef Bay or Eric Lake. Stay right. The terrain is generally flat but can be slippery in some areas.

Boardwalk traverses the wettest sections but expect to scramble over the odd root system and mud hole. Look out for signs of the European settlers, including old telegraph lines and the corduroy road.

· CAMPING: A large campsite is located in the forest at the east side of Eric Lake. It has 11 tent pads, food lockers, and an outhouse. In the campsite, try to stay on the boardwalk to avoid damaging the plant life. Mosquito repellent might be useful at this campsite.

· WATER: There are many creeks and streams along the trail within 1 km (0.6 mi) of Eric Lake. At the campsite, water is available from both the lake and the small stream that feeds into it.

ERIC LAKE TO NELS BIGHT, INCLUDING THE FISHERMAN RIVER CAMPSITE
2.9–16.6 KM (1.8–10.3 MI)—MAP 9

Eric Lake	DISTANCE: 13.7 km (8.5 mi)	Nels Bight
11 tent pads, food lockers, and outhouses	TIME: 5–6 hours DIFFICULTY: Moderate	Beach camping with food lockers and outhouses

BOARDWALK AND FOREST HIKING take you from Eric Lake. The route is flat, but can be muddy and wet. While the terrain is relatively easy, expect a challenge if you plan on hiking from the trailhead to Nels in a single day. As you near Nels Bight and the original Cape Scott settlement, the forest thins and several side trails lead to remnants of the homesteads and farms that once stood here. At 12.8 km (8 mi), you reach a junction in the trail—go left if your destination is Nels Bight or continue straight to Nissen Bight. The trail to Nels Bight continues through the

Hansen Lagoon meadows and back into the forest until you reach the long sandy beach at Nels Bight.

· CAMPING: There are two tent pads and an outhouse at Fisherman River. Nels Bight is the preferred camping destination, providing almost endless beach camping, food lockers, a ranger station, and outhouses.

· WATER: Eric Lake, Fisherman River, and Nels Bight all provide water. Several seasonal creeks are also available.

NELS BIGHT TO CAPE SCOTT LIGHTHOUSE
16.6–23.2 KM (10.3–14.4 MI)—MAP 9

Nels Bight	DISTANCE: 6.6 km (4.1 mi)	Cape Scott lighthouse
Beach camping, food lockers, and outhouses.	TIME: 2.5 hours one way DIFFICULTY: Easy to moderate	Beach camping at Experiment Bight and Guise Bay.

FOR MORE DETAILS ON this weekend backpacking trip, refer to Trail Section 7, page 99.

Shells at Nels Bight.

NISSEN/NELS JUNCTION TO NISSEN BIGHT
12.8-14.5 KM (8-9 MI)—MAP 9

Nissen/Nels junction	DISTANCE: 1.7 km (1.1 mi)	Nissen Bight
Trail crossroads to Nels Bight (west), Nissen Bight (north), or the parking lot (south)	TIME: 0.5 hrs one way DIFFICULTY: Easy	Beach camping with food lockers and outhouses.

FROM THE JUNCTION, GO north towards Nissen Bight along a relatively flat forest trail that follows the old settlers' road. A slight descent down Lard Hill (named by the settlers for its slippery clay soil) takes you to sea level.

· CAMPING: Beach camping is possible the length of Nissen Bight. The west side is the most popular, with both outhouses and a food locker. A second food locker is on the east end of the beach at the trailhead to the North Coast Trail. Water access is at the east side of the beach, 900 m (2,953 ft) from the west entrance. Alternatively, there is a stream 15 minutes south of Nissen.

· WATER: Nissen Bight

NISSEN BIGHT TO LAURA CREEK
14.5-21.5 KM (9-13.4 MI)—MAP 5

Nissen Bight	DISTANCE: 7 km (4.3 mi)	Laura Creek
Beach camping with food lockers and outhouses.	TIME: 3–5 hours DIFFICULTY: Moderate	Forest camping with four tent pads, food lockers, and outhouses.

FROM THE WEST SIDE of Nissen Bight, a staircase takes you into the forest for an inland section. Expect moderate elevation gain as the trail leads to an upland bog plateau, passes Laughing Loon Lake, and skirts around the Nahwitti Cone. The environment is moist and there are several creek crossings. At Dakota Creek the trail begins a gradual descent back to the beach at Laura Creek.

· CAMPING: The Laura Creek campsite is located just inside the forest, and comprises four tent pads, a food locker, and an outhouse. There is also a shelter with a cooking area and benches.

· WATER: Take water from the east side of Nissen Bight, at any of the several creek crossings, or Laura Creek.

LAURA CREEK TO IRONY CREEK (SHUTTLEWORTH BIGHT) 21.5–33.8 KM (13.4–21 MI)—MAP 4

Laura Creek	DISTANCE: 12.3 km (7.6	Irony Creek
Forest camping with	mi)	(Shuttleworth Bight)
four tent pads, food	TIME: 5–7 hours	Beach camping on
lockers, and outhouses	DIFFICULTY: Difficult	Shuttleworth Bight and
		forest camping on four
		tent pads at Irony Creek

BETWEEN LAURA CREEK AND Irony Creek, the trail is predominantly coastal, interspersed with minor forest sections. Cobblestone beaches make for tough terrain, particularly from Laura Creek to Christensen Point. As you near the Strandby River, the trail enters a beautiful forest with easy, riverbed hiking. A cable car provides crossing over Strandby River. Shuttleworth Bight is spectacular and sandy.

135

- CAMPING: Shuttleworth Bight's beach is ideal for camping. The Irony Creek campsite is located at the east side of Shuttleworth Bight just in the forest and comprises four tent pads, a food locker, and an outhouse.

- WATER: Take water from Laura Creek, a small creek just before Christensen Point, a small creek about 1 km (0.6 mi) west of the Strandby River, Strandby River (it can be slightly salty due to tidal currents, especially at high tide), and Irony Creek.

IRONY CREEK (SHUTTLEWORTH BIGHT) TO CAPE SUTIL
33.8–41.0 KM (21–25.5 MI)—MAP 3

Irony Creek (Shuttleworth Bight) Beach camping on Shuttleworth Bight and forest camping on four tent pads at Irony Creek.	DISTANCE: 7.2 km (4.5 mi) TIME: 4–6 hours DIFFICULTY: Difficult	**Cape Sutil** Sandy beach camping in the small bay at Cape Sutil. A ranger station is located here.

THIS SECTION IS CHARACTERIZED by extensive beach hiking on cobblestones, pebbles, and giant beds of seaweed. Rewards include stunning coastline views and hidden pocket beaches. Rainforest trails connect the beaches and, in some places, both beach and forest route options are available. Buoys mark the entrances to inland routes. In the forest, expect steep scrambles with ropes to assist in some locations. A Park Facility Operator station is located at Cape Sutil. The Nahwitti Reserve is located on the cape, which is the northern tip of Vancouver Island. Please do not trespass on this land. As you near Cape Sutil, pay special attention to the buoys marking the forest trail that skirts over the cape to the campsite (if you continue along the beach, you will be trespassing on the Nahwitti Indian Reserve).

- CAMPING: Cape Sutil offers beautiful sandy beach camping, a food locker, and an outhouse.

- WATER: Take water from Irony Creek, several seasonal streams, and at Cape Sutil.

CAPE SUTIL TO NAHWITTI RIVER
41–46.6 KM (25.5–29 MI)—MAP 2

➡️

Cape Sutil	DISTANCE: 5.6 km (3.4 mi)	Nahwitti River
Sandy beach camping in the small bay at Cape Sutil. A ranger station is located here.	TIME: 4–5.5 hours DIFFICULTY: Difficult to very difficult	Forest camping on four tent pads, a food locker, and outhouses.

TIDE TABLES ARE STRONGLY recommended for this section. Tripod Beach, located just west of Long Leg Hill, is impassable at high tide.

This section is characterized by cobblestone beaches, rocky headlands, and tough forest trails. Be prepared for steep forest climbing and rope work. Several pocket beaches are linked by forest trails. After Cape Sutil (just west of Long Leg Hill) is a beach that is impassable at high tide—check tide tables and time your hike accordingly. Over 250 stairs lead up Long Leg Hill and a difficult forest section. The inland trail descends to the Nahwitti River basin and a cable car traverses the water for the final stretch to the Nahwitti River campsite.

- CAMPING: The Nahwitti River campsite is just within the forest and has a food locker, an outhouse, and four tent pads. With gravel and cobblestones, beach camping is not a good option.

- WATER: Take water from a stream at Cape Sutil, a stream just west of Long Leg Hill, a stream 1 km (0.6 mi) west of the cable car, and Nahwitti River above the tidal mixing zone.

NAHWITTI RIVER TO SKINNER CREEK
46.6–48.9 KM (29–30.4 MI)—MAP 2

Nahwitti River	DISTANCE: 2.3 km (1.4 mi)	Skinner Creek
Forest camping comprising four tent pads, food lockers, and outhouses.	TIME: 1–1.5 hours DIFFICULTY: Easy	Beach camping with food lockers and outhouses.

TIDE TABLES ARE RECOMMENDED for this section.

This section is short and relatively easy, with the exception of a couple of scrambles. From Nahwitti River, walk east along the cobblestone beach for about 500 m (1,640 ft) until it leads into the forest. Here, you'll find sturdy ladders, ropes, roots, and not much muck. When you reach the next beach at Skinner Creek you can choose whether to continue through along the beach or take a forest route. The beach is slightly faster and easier; however, at very high tides it can be dangerous or impassable. The forest trail takes you along the ridge parallel to Skinner Beach, passing by remnants of old homesteads. The beach and forest routes converge after about 1 km (0.6 mi) at Skinner Creek campsite.

· CAMPING: Skinner Creek has excellent beach camping, a food locker, and an outhouse.

· WATER: Take water from Nahwitti River (be sure to pull water high on the river to avoid the tidal mixing areas of the estuary) and Skinner Creek.

SKINNER CREEK TO SHUSHARTIE BAY
48.9–57.6 KM (30.4–35.8 MI)—MAP 1

Skinner Creek	DISTANCE: 8.7 km (5.4 mi)	Shushartie Bay
Beach camping with food lockers and outhouses.	TIME: 5–7 hours DIFFICULTY: Moderate to difficult	Forest camping with four tent pads, a food locker, and outhouse. Pack in water.

AN EXCLUSIVELY INLAND SECTION that is neither scenic nor easy but offers an opportunity to view a unique upland bog ecosystem. From sea to a 247-m (810-ft) summit and back down to sea. Expect extensive boardwalk, ladders, rope, mud, and rugged sections. Shushartie Bay is the western trailhead—this is where you meet the water taxi for pick-up/drop-off.

· CAMPING: Shushartie Bay has forest camping 50 m (164 ft) from the trailhead access. There are four tent pads, a food locker, and outhouse. There is also a shelter with a cooking area and benches.

· WATER: Skinner Creek is the only good water source. Pack in water for your hike and if you plan on spending the night at Shushartie Bay campsite, as there is no water supply.

HUMAN HISTORY AND CULTURE OF THE CAPE SCOTT AREA

THIS CHAPTER BEGINS WITH a thank you and an apology. The thank you is for those who generously gave their time to help relay a better understanding of this area's past. It is also meant for people I never met but who, in various ways, helped to preserve stories from the past. The apology is for all that I have missed—and it is likely much. The history of what we today call Cape Scott is as dense and rich as its physical landscape. This is not a history book, but I hope that this brief account promotes a greater understanding, respect, and appreciation for footsteps that walked here before us. For more historical details, please see page 232 for references.

Cape Scott is remote and wild, but has a surprisingly long and varied human history. Most well known amongst this history is the remarkable story of the Cape Scott settlement. This chapter will offer a look at the First Nations of this area, its colonization, settlement, and conservation and protection.

Cape Scott Area Timelines

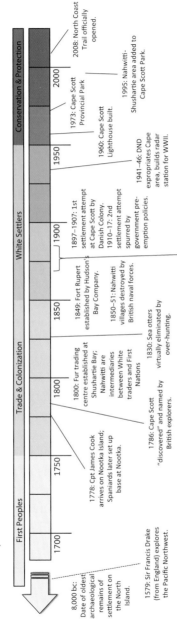

First Peoples	Trade & Colonization	White Settlers	Conservation & Protection

1700

1750

1800

1850

1900

1950

2000

8,000 bc: Date of oldest archaeological remains of settlement on the North Island.

1579: Sir Francis Drake (from England) explores the Pacific Northwest.

1778: Cpt James Cook arrives on Nootka Island; Spaniards later set up base at Nootka.

1786: Cape Scott "discovered" and named by British explorers.

1800: Fur trading centre established at Shushartie Bay; Nahwitti are intermediaries between White traders and First Nations

1830: Sea otters virtually eliminated by over-hunting.

1849: Fort Rupert established by Hudson's Bay Company.

1850–51: Nahwitti villages destroyed by British naval forces.

1897–1907: 1st settlement attempt at Cape Scott by Danish Colony. 1910–17: 2nd settlement attempt spurred by government pre-emption policies.

1871: Under the "Terms of Union" that defined BC's place in the Canadian Confederation, Native peoples became a federal "responsibility." *Indian Act* reduced Native people to the status of legal minors.
1881: Kwawkewlth Agency established. The Kwakwaka'wakw were informed that the function of the Agent was to "tell what it is best for them to do and to look after them as a father would his children" (McKenna-McBride Royal Commission 1916)

1941–46: DND expropriates Cape area, builds radar station for WWII.

1960: Cape Scott Lighthouse built.

1973: Cape Scott Provincial Park

1995: Nahwitti-Shushartie area added to Cape Scott Park.

2008: North Coast Trail officially opened.

FIRST PEOPLES

Ever since the white people first came to our lands, we have been known as the Kwakkewlths by Indian Affairs or as the Kwakiutl by anthropologists. In fact we are the Kwakwaka'wakw, people who speak Kwak'wala, but who live in different places and have different names for our separate groups.

—U'MISTA CULTURAL SOCIETY

THE KWAKWAKA'WAKW

ONE OF THE OLDEST archaeological sites so far found on Vancouver Island is near Port Hardy at Bear Cove and dates back to 8000 BC. The descendants of these people live on today. Cape Scott lies within the traditional territory of the Kwakwaka'wakw (pronounced "kwa kwa ka wak") peoples. Their range stretched from northern Vancouver Island to the adjacent mainland of British Columbia (see map next page). This map delineates tribal boundaries, but it should be noted that these lines were not static. Particularly during the 18th and 19th centuries, these boundaries shifted and changed due to a variety of contributing factors including tribal warfare and mergers, and interactions with European settlers.

At the north end of the island, important village sites and areas of habitation included Khatis at the head of Shushartie Bay, the fortified principal village of Nahwitti at Cape Sutil, the village and fishing station of Go'saa at Shuttleworth Bight, Xwamdasbe at Hope Island, Fisherman Bay, Hansen Bay, Ouchton at Cape Scott/Guise Bay, Semach at Sea Otter Cove, and at the mouth of the San Josef River. Various archaeological sites have been noted within the park, including burial grounds, shell middens, a fish trap, and pictographs.

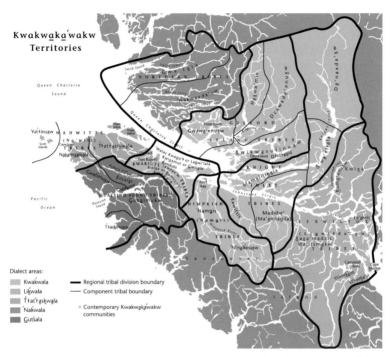

Traditional Kwakwaka'wakw territory. *Reproduced with permission of the U'mista Cultural Centre*

Amongst the Kwakwaka'wakw, there are dialectical differences from community to community and each tribe considers itself distinct. Three tribes inhabited the region that is now Cape Scott Provincial Park—the Tłatłasikwala, the Nakamgilisala, and the Yutlinuk. Circa 1775, tribal boundaries were generally organized as follows: the Yutlinuk inhabited Cox and Lanz Islands, the Nakamgilisala territory extended from east of Sutil to the Cape Scott area, and the Tłatłasikwala inhabited the northwest side from Shushartie Bay to just east of Cape Sutil (including Hope and Nigei Islands).

These tribes faced many challenges, including raids by northern First Nations peoples, environmental hardship, and diseases introduced by Europeans. Over time, these trials led to severe population decline and tribal mergers. By the early 1800s, it is thought that the Yutlinuk were virtually extinct and any remaining members merged with the Nakamgilisala. European traders visiting Shushartie Bay in the early 1820s noted a significant decline in the native population, most likely caused by raids by other tribes. Between the 1830s and the 1850s, the Tsimshian and the Bella Bella carried out a number of raids on the area. John Dunn, writing of the mid-1830s commented that the "Newetee [had been] reduced to a skeleton of its former self, from the inroads of the savages who come from the northern and eastern continent [mainland] to kidnap them, when on their fishing excursions, and then enslave them." (Galois 1994)

The Nakamgilisala and the Tłatłas̱ik̲wa̱la worked together against their common enemies and, in 1855, a particularly devastating raid and massacre prompted the two tribes to merge. They moved to Hope Island (called X̱wa̱mdasbe) and by the end

The village of Xumptaspi on Hope Island; general view from east end. *Image AA-00089 courtesy of Royal BC Museum, BC Archives*

of the 1870s, these people were collectively referred to as the Nahwitti by the Department of Indian Affairs. Today, a small family of Tłatłasikwala lives on Hope Island at Bull Harbour.

Other tribes have traditional territory within and around the Cape Scott area, including the Quatsino and the Kwakiutl (represented by green and orange on the map). These people maintain a significant presence in the North Island region today.

WAY OF LIFE

Historically, the Kwakwaka'wakw were a hunting and gathering society, relying on both marine and land food sources. Throughout the Cape Scott area were villages, trails, hunting routes, and sites of resource gathering, trading, and sacred and ceremonial practices. Legends, seasonal patterns of living, beliefs, and cultural identities were intertwined with and reflected a deep respect for nature.

Central to the Kwakwaka'wakw's subsistence lifestyle was the annual round, a seasonal migration pattern of foraging that was dictated by the availability of food and resources at particular times and places. So fundamental was this annual round that months or moons were mostly named after the sought-after resource or for the occupation that the resource dictated.

Kwakwaka'wakw society was primarily organized according to kinship and a hierarchical rank system that ranged from nobility to slaves. Each tribal group had a distinct traditional territory, and was composed of several hierarchically ranked kin-groups called numayms,

Polly of Shushartie Bay. *Image H-05510 courtesy of Royal BC Museum, BC Archives*

145

POTLATCH AND THE NORTH ISLAND FIRST NATIONS

A potlatch is a gift-giving feast and significant cultural event practised by indigenous peoples of the Pacific Northwest coast. Traditionally, winter provided a time for feasts, gathering, ceremonies, and relationship-building among and within tribes. It was an important time to solidify relationships and further develop social and economic order. Potlatches were the primary economic system and included songs and elaborate dances that reflected genealogy, wealth, and legend. The families that distributed the most gifts, including animal skins, storable foods such as eulachon, and canoes raised their status.

Potlatches were made illegal in Canada in 1884, largely as a result of missionaries and government agents who considered it wasteful, unproductive, and contrary to "civilized," European values. The ban was repealed in 1951 and the Kwakwa̱ka̱'wakw continue the practice today.

roughly translated to mean "those of one kind." Members of numayms claimed descent from a common ancestor, usually in the form of an animal and place of origin. Social rank dictated which families had access to particular resource sites, camps, or other privileges. Specific activities and movements varied from tribe to tribe (for example, the Nahwitti focussed on halibut, and the Quatsino people hunted humpback and minke whales).

Around the end of November, several different numayms would gather together as a single tribe in their principal winter village site (the Nahwitti village at Cape Sutil was one of these villages). As the cold and wet winter set in, a season of feasting, potlatches, and ceremonies began. Winter was also spent visiting other tribes. Every numaym occupied houses in its own section of the village and sponsored its own potlatches and ceremonial dances.

When spring arrived, the tribes dispersed in smaller family groups to their seasonal camping spots, and fishing, hunting, and gathering places. For the Kwakwa̱ka'wakw, thinking and relating to the land was complex and involved the knowledge of family claims to the land, together with the knowledge of the land's resources and how to use them. (Galois 1994)

LEGEND

The earliest histories of the Kwakwa̱ka'wakw are recorded in the creation stories and ancestral histories passed down through generations of oral traditions. This is one of the Tłatła̱siḵwa̱la legends shared by the U'mista Cultural Centre:

X̱WA̱MDASBE (HOPE ISLAND)
Edward Dossetter, 1891, American Museum of Natural History
(Adapted from Boas and Hunt, Kwakiutl Texts, 1905–6)

As the Creator was going about changing things into the way they are today, he spent much time making the animals. One of the first animals that he created was the mink. Creator was at a place called South-side-beach when he saw a very small man sharpening a spear with a long handle. The Creator asked, "What are you doing?" And the little man replied that he was sharpening his long spear to fight the Creator with. "Let me see that," the Creator said. And taking the spear, he drove it into the Mink where he sits down, saying, "There. It is better there, and you will wear it as a tail in later generations." He also made raccoon this way, for raccoon was sharpening a striped spear, hoping to fight Creator with it. Thus, raccoon has a striped tail and a mask on his face today. Deer's horns here placed there by

Creator, too. Deer was sitting at Shouting-place sharpening up mussel-shell knives when the Creator came by. Deer didn't recognize Creator and confided in this stranger that he was intending to kill the Creator with his sharp knives. Well, Creator stuck the knives on deer's head; and they are still there today as antlers.

The Creator was continually on the move, for the world in those days needed a lot of changing to make the world as we see it today. He created all of the tribes of the world, as well. But, then, one day he was at a place called Clover-roots-at-mouth-of-river and he noticed a woman called Yaxagama who was so beautiful that he could not leave her. He was stopped there for some time, and their children became the ancestors of the Nakamgilisala.

EXPLORATION, TRADE AND COLONIZATION

EARLY EXPLORATION AND TRADE

While First Nations peoples have called it home for centuries, the Pacific Northwest was largely unknown to the rest of the world until the mid-1700s. At this time, Russian, Spanish, American, and British explorers began probing BC's coast in search of wealth through new resources and opportunities to expand colonial frontiers. By the late 18th century, exploration and trade on North Vancouver Island (and elsewhere along BC's coast) began in earnest, fuelled by competition and a colonial agenda to discover, map, name, claim, and exploit whatever valued resources possible.

In 1786, Cape Scott was "discovered" by British explorers Captain John Guise and Captain Henry Lowrie, aboard their respective ships, the *Experiment* and *Captain Cook*. They named the cape after David Scott, one of the main financial supporters of that year's trading voyage. Guise Bay, Experiment Bight, and the

Scott Islands also carry names from this voyage. When Lowrie and Guise stopped in San Josef Bay and Sea Otter Cove, they saw no inhabitants but noted clear evidence of fishing activity by the First Nations.

In 1792, the *Columbia*, an American ship, explored the Quatsino Sound area and did encounter First Nations people. Many canoes came alongside the ship and the following account was recorded by John Boit:

> *They was all dressed in War Armour, and completely arm'd with Bows, arrows, and Spears, and had altogether quite a savage appearance. I believe they was fearfull we shou'd rob their village, which was at no great distance as they appear'd much agitated. however soon began a brisk trade for Otter furts. We landed with the baots and Got Wood and Broom Stuff, but the Indians wishing to be troublesome, soon give over this business. indeed I was obliged to knock one of them down with my Musket* [sic]. *(Howay 1941)*

WHILE EARLY INTERACTIONS WERE uncertain, tenuous, and even violent, for the most part, the relationships between early traders and First Nations appeared mutually cooperative, with both parties motivated to get what the other offered. Various ship records made note of the First Nations people being experienced, savvy, and highly competitive in their trade dealings.

FUR TRADE ON THE NORTH ISLAND

BY THE EARLY 19TH century, contact between white traders (European, American, and Russian) and First Nations was frequent. Trade in furs—particularly sea otter pelts, which fetched high prices in China—was the basis for these interactions. Competition to secure strategic trade advantage was fierce, both among First Nations tribes and white traders. Britain eventually gained dominance and, through the Hudson's Bay Company, secured its commercial interests in the area.

The fur trade brought a variety of negative effects. The First Nations people were exposed to smallpox and tuberculosis, to which they had no immunity. This contact process has been called a "demographic disaster" for the Kwakwaka'wakw—when historic numbers were compared to a 1924 census, it was estimated that population had been reduced by a staggering 90 percent. Participation in the fur trade also brought irreversible effects on aboriginal culture: competition for trade advantage was a catalyst for inter-tribal conflict and the introduction of alcohol, guns, and other elements of European culture over just a few decades changed traditional ways of life that had existed for millennia. The fur trade was also devastating for local wildlife. Such was the volume of trade that by 1830, sea otters were virtually extinct along the Pacific Northwest coast. Conservation efforts to reverse this and its resultant effect on the food chain continue to this day. When the supply of sea otters dwindled, the fur trade shifted its focus to beaver and marten pelts.

In the early trader days, the First Nations village of Nahwitti was a favourite port of call, especially amongst the American traders. The location provided wealth and strategic advantage for the Nahwitti people. Around 1800, Shushartie Bay became the primary trading centre, favoured by trading ships for its protected bay. While the Nahwitti village lost its importance, the Tłatłasikwala were able to maintain their tactical position at Shushartie Bay, where they acted as middlemen to other tribes seeking to trade their furs.

In 1821, the British government sought to consolidate its trading power—it forced the North West Company to merge with the Hudson's Bay Company (HBC), allowing the HBC to increase

DID YOU KNOW?

To maintain a speed of 6 knots (11 km or around 7 mi per hour), the Beaver burned about one tonne (over 1,000 kg) of coal every hour!

its activity and expand its fur trading empire within British Columbia. The HBC set about establishing a series of forts along the Pacific coast in an effort to eliminate American competition. As a consequence of this shifting power dynamic, the importance of the Shushartie Bay post began to wane. When the *Beaver* steamship began operation in 1836 and allowed access to previously inaccessible parts of the coast, Shushartie Bay closed down. The *Beaver* surpassed the power and manoeuvrability of earlier vessels, and functioned as a floating trading post and connection between HBC ports from the Columbia River to Alaska.

The next major development in the area occurred in 1849 when, motivated to secure rights over nearby coal, the HBC built Fort Rupert. Located at the site of Tsaxis, an old Kwakiutl village about 10 km (6.2 mi) south from where Port Hardy is today, Fort Rupert was North Vancouver Island's first permanent European settlement. While coal mining was the primary interest, Fort Rupert also served as a trading post that allowed the company to take full control over the influx of goods and supplies. Kwakiutl tribes flocked to the area and consolidated into a single winter village outside the log walls to secure an intermediary role in the fur trade, as well as rights to the coal mining.

THE NAHWITTI INCIDENTS OF 1850 AND 1851

In July 1850, a California-bound vessel stopped at Fort Rupert to collect coal. On board were four stowaways who had deserted the HBC from another vessel. Fearing capture, three of them fled into the surrounding wilderness. Not long after, word spread that the stowaways had been murdered at a nearby Nahwitti village. The HBC fort was facing growing tensions in its relations with both the miners and the Kwakiutl and did not want to create greater instability. The company also lacked adequate resources for enforcement. Instead of retaliation for the deaths of the men, fort magistrate John Sebastian Helmcken wrote to Governor Blanshard appealing for help: "If we make no demonstration the Indians will lose all respect for us and make an attack upon our fort..." (Sellers 2003)

Blanshard responded and sailed from Victoria to Fort Rupert that October aboard the *Daedalus*. Before taking military action, Helmcken approached the Nahwitti village and demanded surrender of the murderers. He reported that "the chiefs said they could not, but were willing to pay the value of the murdered men in blankets, furs, or any goods, according to their custom." In response to this, Blanshard demanded that the Nahwitti be taught a lesson: "The Queen's name is a tower of strength, but at Fort Rupert it apparently requires to be backed with the Queen's bayonets." The British Navy sailed to the Nahwitti village. They found the village deserted but burned it to the ground. This was the first use of military force against an aboriginal community on Vancouver Island.

Teaching the First Nations a lesson and proving the dominance of British authority and law was a primary concern for Blanshard. Not satisfied with the message sent by the destruction of an empty village, Blanshard returned the following year aboard the *Daphne*, a warship. They arrived at the Cape Sutil village with sixty armed sailors and exchanged shots with the Nahwitti. Several villagers were killed or wounded before the Nahwitti fled to Sea Otter Cove. Again, the British destroyed the village. Shortly afterwards, some of the Nahwitti arrived at Fort Rupert and relinquished the bodies of three men who they claimed were the killers. The Nahwitti survivors later moved to Bull Harbour on nearby Hope Island. Although it is a First Nations reserve today, Cape Sutil remains uninhabited.

The Nahwitti incident was a key element in a shift from relatively cooperative relations between First Nations and Europeans to one of dominance and control. Not limited to the North Island, this happened across the province (and elsewhere in the continent) and included the establishment of missionary and residential schools, the abolishment of cultural traditions, the creation of the reserve system, and other strategies to marginalize the rights of aboriginal people. In 1871, under the Terms of the

U'MISTA CULTURAL CENTRE

The U'mista's Cultural Centre is in the village of Alert Bay on Cormorant Island. Its exhibits tell the stories of the Kwakwa̱ka̱'wakw and pay particular attention to the ritual of potlatch. Since a time beyond memory, the Kwakwa̱ka̱'wakw have hosted potlatches and the ceremony continues to play a central and unifying role in the community today. The potlatch was banned in Canada between 1885 and 1951 and the masks and other regalia that you can see in the Big House Gallery at U'mista were all surrendered under duress after an illegal potlatch in 1921. After the ban was lifted, the Kwakwa̱ka̱'wakw people negotiated for decades for the return of their sacred regalia, which was scattered in museums and private collections around the world. Most of the confiscated regalia has come home and can be seen at the U'mista Cultural Centre and at the Nuyumbalees Museum in Cape Mudge, near Campbell River. The word *u'mista* is Kwak'wala and means "the return of something important." The return of the Kwakwa̱ka̱'wakw's stolen treasures is a form of u'mista.

Union, which defined BC's place in the Canadian confederation, Native peoples became a federal responsibility. The 1876 federal *Indian Act* reduced Native people to the status of legal minors. In 1881, the Kwawkewlth Agency was established and the Kwakwaka'wakw were informed that the function of the Indian Agent was to "tell what it is best for them to do and to look after them as a father would his children" (McKenna-McBride Royal Commission 1916). The potlatch was banned in 1885, under revisions to the *Indian Act*. Much more could be written about the hardships and injustices suffered as a result of the *Indian Act* and other actions that sought to assimilate and control First Nations. Please see the list of recommended reading on page 235.

The late 19th and early 20th century marked the beginning of a new chapter in Cape Scott's history. Commercial interest dwindled when gold and other mining prospects showed more promise elsewhere in BC. Some coal miners remained, as did the First Nations, but the era of the North Island fur trade was officially over. Fort Rupert was established for commercial motives—for fur and resource exploitation—but increasing numbers of immigrants now came to Canada in search of a new homeland. By this time period, most Native people were thought to have left the Cape Scott region. Contact with these new settlers was minor, but there is a record of some conflict for land and resources with aboriginals.

WHITE SETTLEMENT
In 1894, a Seattle-based Danish immigrant named Rasmus Hansen came across the Cape Scott area while out fishing. Rasmus anchored his fishing boat in Goose Harbour (now Hansen Bay) and found fertile-looking meadows and streams full of salmon. The seed of an idea was planted and, encouraged by Canadian immigration policies instituting a "new system of colonization by the formation of colonies," Hansen and several prospective colonists wrote to the government with a request to farm the

land and a proposed settlement plan. The provincial government approved, provided that at least 30 settlers could be obtained. The government also committed to build a road from Fisherman Bay to San Josef River and on to Holberg. This road would provide a critical transportation link and help the settlers get their goods to market.

One of the prospective colonists, Nels C. Nelson, spent the winter of 1896–97 living alone at the proposed colony site, making rudimentary shelters for the coming settlers and building rough trails. In the meantime, founders of the colony began writing letters to Danish-language newspapers and holding meetings to entice prospective colonists with promising stories of an idyllic settlement, abundant resources, and independence to live off the land.

1897–1907: A DANISH COLONY

As a result of these efforts, the years from 1897 to 1907 marked the first white settlement attempt at Cape Scott. Most of this

Early Settlers, c.1902. L to R: N.C. Nelson; Lars Jensen (N.P. Jensen's son); Carl Rasmussen; Simmy Simonsen; Theodore Frederiksen. *From the collection of Ruth Botel*

Collecting the mail at Fisherman's Bay. Some settlers walked 8 km
(5 mi) to collect mail. *From the collection of Ruth Botel with thanks to
Anna Frederiksen*

centered around Fisherman Bay and the meadows of Hansen
Lagoon. The intent was to subsist by farming and fishing until
the promised road was built. The settlers were Danish and Dan-
ish-American families and single men from Minnesota, Iowa,
Nebraska, and North Dakota. In just one year, the population of
the Cape Scott colony numbered 90 people.

Fierce storms and poor harbour conditions prevented the
construction of a dock, and only a muddy and rugged route
known as the London Trail linked Cape Scott with communities further south on Vancouver Island. The settlers toiled
tirelessly for several years. With the help of Carl Rasmussen's steam-powered sawmill, they built many homesteads, a
church, school, and a community hall by hand. A cooperative
store and post office was established at Fisherman Bay. They

HOMEMADE LANTERNS

A homemade lantern made by settlers from a tin can was known as a bug. These lanterns were hung on a tree limb near rivers, the candle flame protected from the breeze by the can. Extra candles ("bugs") were packed by travellers.

A re-creation of the bug lantern, used by settlers at night. *Photo: Ruth Botel*

also built trails, wagon roads, and, when the monthly steamer service was deemed insufficient, their own boats. The *Cape Scott* provided a decade of service from 1901 before she was lost to the sea, joining a long list of other vessels that have sunk in these treacherous waters.

The meadows were considered a backbone of the colony so one of the first major projects was a dyke to keep the saltwater tides out. The massive undertaking took several months, and was planned by N.P. Jensen and mostly built by him and a team of horses. When completed in 1899, it stretched about 700 m (2,300 ft) across the mouth of the Fisherman River. While the community celebrated the dyke's completion, a storm raged. The next morning, the settlers found that the dyke had been washed away, likely due to Jensen's insistence that the sluice gates be shut before the soil and rocks had settled. The settlers attempted another dyke, this time at a location more protected from direct tides. The second dyke was completed in 1905, but unfortunately the sluice gates never effectively held the water in or out.

Every month, a steamship would come into Fisherman Bay to bring supplies. With no wharf, it was difficult to load and unload cargo. Animals were lowered by sling or pushed overboard and forced to swim. Supplies were paddled ashore on small dories or rafts and then packed home.

Without a road to supply their own goods to market, many of the settlers turned to fishing as a source of income. In mid-June the men would set out by foot and boat for Rivers Inlet, not returning until the end of August. Finding that fishing wasn't adequate income, some travelled by rowboat to work in mines or logging camps elsewhere on Vancouver Island. Others made money by trapping. Most of the settlers' protein came from fishing—trout, salmon, and crabs—and hunting. A variety of wild berries were also plentiful.

Community meetings were held in the church, which also housed the first school. The well-liked teacher, "Professor" Carl Christensen, lived upstairs until he completed his own home nearby. Christensen was an influential figure and leader in the community. In addition to being the colony's teacher, he created the Sandfly community newspaper and, when Rasmus Hansen left the village, became the community leader.

William Christensen's grave at Cape Scott. It reads "William, Adopted son of C.B. Christensen, Died Oct 17 1906, Aged 12 years 5 mos; The sun went down while it was yet day." William died of tetanus.

158

Henry Ohlsen at work in his store.
Image A-09469 courtesy of Royal BC Museum, BC Archives

To bring the enrollment number up to the minimum required for a new school, Christensen adopted seven-year-old William (and later adopted three other children). While working on a secret birthday present for his father, William stepped on a rusty nail but did not tell anyone. The wound became fatally infected with tetanus and Carl buried him in their yard. A large marble monument was brought in to mark William's grave and can still be seen today. The lonely stone is a testament to the bittersweet struggles, isolation, and fortitude that these people faced.

Life was hard for the settlers. Severe weather, dangerous nautical conditions, sudden storms, isolation, insufficient transportation, and limited supplies created adversity that few modern Canadians have ever contended with. Yet there was apparently rarely a feeling of hardship or complaint, and those who later recounted memories spoke fondly of their time at Cape Scott. Celebrations were common, whether Christmas dinners, summer picnics, or dances at Eric Lake.

But as the years passed and the promises of a road were never fulfilled, disappointment grew. A government telegraph line provided communications to the area, but there was still no way to get supplies in or out in an efficient manner. The provincial government, perhaps fearing a backlash for establishing a "little Denmark," not only refused to grant any additional land leases, but also failed to issue land titles promised to colonists who had resided on and developed the land for the requisite five years.

In 1907, two key events sealed the fate of the already-struggling colony. The first was the elimination of the steamship service to

Fisherman Bay, in part due to perceived rudeness of the settlers to the ship crew, who considered their service to Cape Scott a favour. As a consequence, the general store was forced to relocate to Holberg in early 1909, where supplies were more dependable. The second was when the BC government, in hope of encouraging population growth and a greater cultural mix, set aside a section of Crown land from the head of Quatsino Sound to Cape Scott for pre-emption to individual land-seekers. Pre-emption was a method of acquiring vacant, un-reserved Crown land by claiming it for cultivation. Individuals could apply to settle and "improve" the land and then acquire the land through purchase at a discount rate or at no further charge. A Crown grant was issued and ownership of the land passed into private hands.

Faced with uncertainty, inadequate transportation, and limited income opportunities, the colony dissolved and disbanded. With hopes for a more sustainable future, some moved to surrounding fishing and logging communities like Holberg and Quatsino, while others headed south to pre-empt

TRAVEL TIMES FOR SETTLERS (APPROXIMATE)

BY BOAT — FISHERMAN BAY TO:
- Shushartie Bay: 4 hours
- Rivers Inlet: 9 hours
- Quatsino Village to San Josef Bay: 7 hours

BY TRAIL — SAN JOSEF BAY TO:
- Sea Otter Cove: 3.5 hours
- Cape Scott Settlement:: 4 hours
- Holberg: 4.5 hours

Hansen Lagoon to Shushartie Bay: 2 days (overnight at Shuttleworth's house at Strandby River)

land around San Josef Bay. By 1909, there were fewer than 60 people left near the cape. But the place names persist—Nels Bight, Hansen Lagoon, Frederiksen Point, Eric Lake, and others remind us of the Danish colony's dream.

1910–1917: SECOND SETTLEMENT ATTEMPT

Land pre-emption opportunities spurred the second major settlement attempt of the Cape Scott area. By 1912, more than 600 people had arrived to the area. Most of them were from Washington State, the prairie and eastern provinces of Canada, and Europe. Unlike the Danish colony, most new arrivals operated as individuals under the government's new pre-emption laws. Many occupied homesteads vacated by the Danes. Others took land and built new homes at San Josef Bay, Shuttleworth Bight, and Shushartie Bay. This small-scale land rush took the population to its peak of 1,000 in 1913. A government surveyor reported the San Josef valley to be one of the most fertile areas of the province—a description that undoubtedly encouraged more settlers to flock to the area.

By 1914, a church, post office, and community hall/school had been established near Hansen Lagoon. At its peak, about 30 students of various backgrounds attended the school. The Strandby River area was also attractive to settlers and by 1915 a store, church, post office, and one-room school were also located at the mouth of the river. The settlers had a strong community spirit and combated isolation with dances, fairs, and regular meetings.

Trails were rugged and often too treacherous for horses. This meant that supplies—whether flour, canned milk, oatmeal, sugar, tools, or even stoves—were carried by foot. The standard pack for an able-bodied man was 110 lbs (with no hip belts or cushioning!). One story passed down recounts that of a brother and sister who, with fully loaded packs, trekked the 6.4 km (4 mi) journey home from the store. The brother scolded his sister for forgetting a 50-lb sack of flour.

Some of the settlers outside the Cape Scott community hall/school house during Fall Fair, c. 1915. People from Holberg, San Josef Bay, Sea Otter Cove, and Cape Scott attended the event. *From the collection of Ruth Botel with thanks to the Wadey family*

In response, she opened the door of the stove she was carrying to reveal the sack of flour inside!

Despite such tales of fortitude, it didn't take long for the climate, inadequate transportation, and lack of income to dampen the settlers' enthusiasm. The population began dwindling and in 1917 World War I marked an official beginning-of-the-end to the second settlement attempt. In 1917 the population numbered 150. By 1923, there were just 50 people left in the area. Those not conscripted for service in the war either went back to their place of origin or found work in the resource industries elsewhere on Vancouver Island. While the area was nearly abandoned, a few hardy souls persisted. Alfred Spencer was one of the last remaining settlers. He had arrived in 1921 and farmed on the north side of the Hansen Lagoon road, before finally leaving the cape in 1956.

What was not worth packing out was left behind. Today, rusting remnants of stoves and farm equipment, wagon roads paved with logs, dilapidated buildings, and moss-cloaked graves can still be found.

WORLD WAR II

While World War I prompted an exodus, World War II triggered a short-lived influx of people and activity. In 1941 the Department of National Defense (DND) sought to bolster their coastal defenses and identified Cape Scott as a strategic location to protect national security and detect Japanese war planes. The DND took over the Cape Scott area and built a radar station and small military base. Most of the air force lived in tents, although the Frederiksen family had their home expropriated to serve as quarters for the officers. The Frederiksens were required to report their destination to the military every time they left the property. Fifty men were stationed in the area until the base closed in 1946. During this time, an airport was also built at Fort Rupert. Here, an enormous bank of clamshells—3.2 km (2 mi) long, 0.8 km (0.5 mi) wide and around 15 m (50 ft) high—was used to level the airport. The shells were the last vestiges of First Nations feasts held here for generations.

In 1960, the Cape Scott lighthouse was built as one of three lighthouse stations constructed in response to increased marine vessel traffic from the new Alcan smelter in Kitimat. Some of the old radar buildings from World War II were re-used and new residences were constructed for the keepers. The lighthouse remains staffed today and is operated by the Canadian Coast Guard.

CONSERVATION AND PROTECTION

In 1971, in celebration of BC's centennial, Holberg Ground Search and Rescue cleared some of the settlers' roads at Cape Scott. This accessibility had unfortunate consequences—the remaining homesteads (some of which still had coats hanging in them) were looted and several were burnt to the ground. In 1973, Cape Scott Provincial Park was established to protect over 15,054 ha (37,200 acres) and to "to preserve its wilderness quality and the essence of the area's cultural heritage."

More than 20 years later, the area from Nahwitti River to Shushartie Bay was officially identified as a coastal corridor that would enhance the park's ability to provide quality wilderness experiences. Totalling 2,732 ha (6,750 acres), this area was added to the park in 1995. Workshops were held to develop a common vision for the park and, driven by community interest, the concept of a North Coast Trail became a major focus.

The desire for economic diversification was a driver for the creation of the North Coast Trail. The resource-focused economy of the North Island has been struggling since the late 20th century and the growing attraction of eco-tourism was seen as an opportunity to attract tourists to North Vancouver Island and showcase the region's natural beauty and history.

From concept to reality, the North Coast Trail is largely credited to the fundraising and lobbying efforts of the Northern

Inaugural hike of the North Coast Trail, November 2007. Left to right: Ben Pawlett, Shaun Korman, Dave Trebett, Ron Quilter, Dave Parker, Jacob Blanchard, Ben McGibbon, and John Lok. *Photo: Strategic Natural Resource Consultants*

THE CARROT CAMPAIGN

Without Highway 19, there would be no North Coast Trail and little other tourism on North Vancouver Island. A lack of reliable transportation routes long affected North Islanders. In 1953, a paved highway was built to connect Nanaimo and Campbell River but the North Island remained accessible only by boat, plane, or gravel logging roads. In the late 1970s, North Island residents launched the Carrot Campaign in an attempt to shame the provincial government into delivering. In 1979, the highway was finally built, and in salute to their victory and in a nod to the setters' struggles in the past, Port Hardy installed a half-chewed wooden carrot in Carrot Park to commemorate the event. The sign by the carrot reads: "This carrot, marking the northern end of the Island highway, is a symbol of government road building promises, dangled in front of North Island settlers since 1897."

Vancouver Island Trails Society (NVITS). Comprised of volunteers from the local communities, the NVITS and other volunteers committed countless hours over almost 15 years into the development of the North Coast Trail.

From 2000 to 2002, the provincial government acquired almost 728 ha (1,800 acres) of private property in the Cape Scott area. In 2004, these lands were added to the park. The same year, the North Coast Trail route was finalized and trail construction began with funding provided by both the federal and provincial governments. At an estimated cost of $1.5 million, the trail was surveyed and constructed by the Strategic Forest Management Company. In May 2008, the North Coast Trail officially opened.

The park continues to be managed and maintained by Strategic Forest Management Company as the Park Facility

Operators. The NVITS is still active and continues to promote the trail and the region's other recreational opportunities.

Today, Cape Scott Provincial Park is a critical component of BC's protected areas network. BC Park's management plan for the park focuses on its cultural, wildlife, and recreational values. It protects unique coastal habitats including sandy beaches, rainforests, lowland bogs, and muskeg. The park is home to a diversity of vegetation and wildlife, including migratory birds and iconic elk, bear, wolves, and cougars. The cultural and historical sites outlined in this book are also integral to the park. As the park becomes more popular, it is important to balance recreational interests with respect and protection of its features.

HISTORICAL PLACES, NAMES AND POINTS OF INTEREST

THE FOLLOWING PROVIDES AN overview of historical names and places of interest within Cape Scott Provincial Park. Numbers on the map correspond with the list of names and descriptions. Where possible, the Kwakwaka'wakw name and translation is provided in parentheses. This glossary has been made possible through information provided by BC Parks, local historian Ruth Botel, and historical texts. The individual Danish homestead sites are too numerous to list but extend throughout the park, particularly around the west side. Please remember that all historical items are a protected part of this park's heritage—do not remove or disturb them.

1. HENRY OHLSEN HOME, store, and post office (1908–1944). Only a few rotting planks and rusting relics remain.

2. SAN JOSEF BAY (Nomx, pron. *numx*). Listed by Mungo Martin as an old village site.

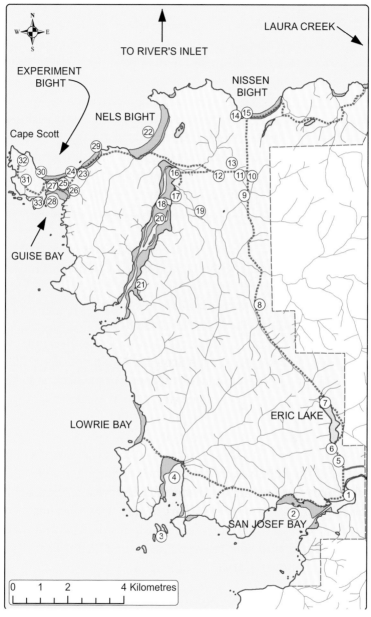

Places of historical interest within Cape Scott and the west side of the park.

3. HELEN ISLAND. Known as Stuttard's Island to the locals. This place "for drink and girls" was a stopover for fishermen travelling the coast. See page 118 for details on proprietor Pansy Mae Stuttard.

4. SEA OTTER COVE (Semach, pron. *simax*). Named after the ship of Captain James Hanna, the *Sea Otter*. This was a favourite camp of the Nakomgilisala for halibut fishing, hunting, and gardening. The Nakomgilisala house was destroyed and the people driven off by white traders about 1910. Later, several settler homesteads were located here.

5. CORDUROY ROAD. Remnants of the 1908 road that connected the south end of Eric Lake with the San Josef store and post office.

6. WHARF. Served as a transportation link during peak years before the trail around the lake was constructed.

7. ERIC LAKE. Named after N.P. Jensen's adopted son Eric Miller, who died in 1910 alongside Lars Jensen when their boat, the *Cape Scott*, sank on a trip to Quatsino with mail and freight.

8. TELEGRAPH LINE. In 1913, telegraph and telephone lines were installed between Sea Otter Cove, Cape Scott, and San Josef Bay. The lines provided communications to Holberg and other outside places. Look out for the old line in open areas along the trail.

9. FARM FENCE POSTS. Wooden fence posts from settler times run parallel to the trail and two sets run perpendicular to the trail through an open bog area.

10. WILLIAM CHRISTENSEN'S GRAVE. A 1.8-m (6-ft) pink granite monument marks the grave of William Christensen, who died of tetanus in 1906, aged 12. See page 158 for more details.

11. WOODEN CART. Located in a meadow off the north side of the trail near Spencer Farm. Alfred Spencer farmed here until 1956.

12. CATERPILLAR TRACTOR. The first motorized machine used at Cape Scott is lodged between two trees on the north side of the trail.

13. COLLAPSED TOOL SHED. Follow the side trail near the Spencer Farm sign.

14. BREAKWATER. The remains of an old sailing vessel that was sunk here to add protection. Unfortunately, it did not survive winter storms and was soon washed ashore.

15. FISHERMAN BAY (bɛk·!â, pron. *ba̲k'a*). Noted as a traditional village and First Nations resource site in "a camp for the purpose of catching and drying their winter's supply of Kawash (halibut)."

16. SECOND DYKE. Completed in 1905, the dyke was built by settlers to claim land for pasture. To spot it, look for the raised shoreline along the northwest shore of Hansen Lagoon.

17. FIRST DYKE. Large mound of rocks runs 720 m (2,362 ft) across the lagoon just east of the middle arm of Fisherman River. Completed in 1899. See page 157 for details on the failed dykes.

18. BOILER. Lodged in the riverbank on the north side of the middle arm of Fisherman River. Used by Jensen for his milk condenser or sawmill circa 1898.

19. FISHERMAN RIVER. Named after one of the first settlers, Nels P. Jensen, who was nicknamed "The Fisherman." Jensen died at the age of 74 in 1934 at Cape Scott. He is buried at Guise Bay. See page 103 for a photograph of his grave.

20. HANSEN LAGOON (Wachalis, meaning "river on the beach in the bay"). Named for the founder of the Danish colony, Rasmus Hansen. The meadows of Hansen Lagoon were the hub of the initial Danish settlement. Remains of homesteads, a community hall and schoolhouse, farm implements, and gravestones can be found here.

21. *KEYAIL*. Here, the Kwakwaka'wakw peoples butchered and dried whale meat for winter food stores.

22. NELS BIGHT (ts!ᵋwǔ'nxas, pron. *t'sạ'wạnxas*, meaning "winter place"). Identified as a point of origin or village of the Koskimo by historian Franz Boas.

23. PLANK ROAD. Constructed in 1942 to transport goods between various World War II buildings.

24. BUILDING RUINS. Follow the small trail off the main trail about 50 m (164 ft) before Guise Bay to see a long rectangular building believed to have been a store during World War II.

25. BUILDING RUINS. Follow a small trail off Guise Bay to see two cabins used as World War II barracks.

26. DRIFTWOOD FENCE POSTS. Half-buried and crooked remains of a driftwood fence running east to west behind Guise Bay. Built by N.P. Jensen in 1910 in an attempt to stabilize the sand dunes for pasture.

27. SAND NECK (or Apdzeges, meaning "against each other"). Once a seasonal camp for First Nations, this sand neck is also believed to be the sight of a major battle between the Quatsino and the Nakamgilisala and is an identified First Nations burial site. About 1910, Danish settler Nels P. Jensen tried to tame the

sand dunes by constructing driftwood fences. The logs were as long as 52 m (16 ft), so this was quite a feat for one man! For a time, the area provided grazing for Jensen's stock. Hay was cut by scythe and collected by horse and buggy. Jensen's grave is located in the grass on the western side of these dunes, bordered by a picket fence at the forest edge. Theodore Frederiksen later owned this land, where he produced crops and grazed cattle. In the sand neck is a wooden A-frame structure used as a cougar trap by the Jensen children. A cougar was actually captured and held for 10 minutes, much to the surprise of the children.

28. GUISE BAY (Patschach).

29. EXPERIMENT BIGHT (Gwigwakawalis, meaning "whales on the beach"). The site of a seasonal village for the Kwakwa̱ka̱'wakw. It is said that you can see the footprint of the Transformer, K'aniki'lakw, pushed into the rocks. Legend has it that K'aniki'lakw was able to step to Triangle Island from here in a single stride. East of Experiment Bight is Yichaledzas, which may mean "where canoes run ashore in heavy swell."

30. NATIVE MIDDEN. Beached shell and bones mark the remnants of a Native food fishing site at the west end of Experiment Bight.

31. PLANK ROAD. Used to transport goods to the lighthouse station.

32. CAPE SCOTT LIGHTHOUSE. Built in 1960.

33. OUCHTON (ăxᵘdɛ'm, meaning "foam place"). Just north of Guise Bay, Ouchton was known as a First Nations fishing and hunting station for seals, sea otters, shellfish, and other resources. It is now a federally designated Indian Reserve.

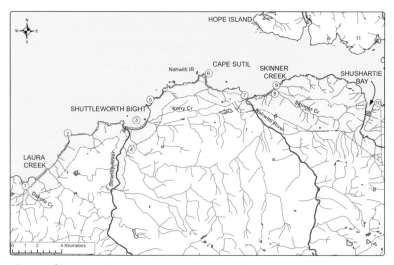

Places of historical interest, Laura Creek to Shushartie Bay and the east side of the park.

1. DAKOTA CREEK (Wachlalis, meaning "river on beach in bay").

2. CHRISTENSEN POINT (Yachbe, meaning "bad point"). Named after the settler teacher, who lived in the vicinity.

3. SHUTTLEWORTH BIGHT (Kosae or Go'saa, pron. *gusa̲'yi* or *guse'* or Kegegwis, meaning "sandy beach"). The unnamed lake just west of the mouth of the Strandby River near Shuttleworth Bight is considered a point of origin of both the Koskimo and Nakomgilisala. It was a village site and a main fishing station. Harry Shuttleworth and his family were early European settlers here. A small pocket of land remains private.

4. STRANDBY RIVER. Formerly called Cache Creek because halibut fishers would cache their goods ashore here. It was also the site of a minor gold rush during the time that prospectors were exploring all areas of BC with a fever for striking it rich.

5. GULYADE (meaning "having abalone"). A bay approximately 0.6 km (1 mi) north of Shuttleworth Bight. Just beyond it is a peninsula known as Techbala (meaning "hanging at the point").

6. CAPE SUTIL (Nahwitti). The area was named Sutil Point in 1792, after the Spanish exploring schooner *Sutil* (meaning "subtle"), which made an examination of the channels between Vancouver Island and the mainland. It was renamed Cape Commerell by the British in 1860 and then reverted back to the Spanish name in 1906. Cape Sutil was the primary village site of the Kwakwaka'wakw before it was shelled and burned by the British naval fleet in 1850 and again in 1851. The villagers fled and many relocated to Hope Island. See page 151 for more details. Today, the northern tip of the cape is a reserve of the Nahwitti First Nation and should not be trespassed upon.

7. NAHWITTI RIVER (Wuda Staade, meaning "having cold water" or Malopa). Historically, the Nahwitti River was a Native village site. Later, it was the location of a European settlement attempt. On the opposite side of the river mouth from the campsite are old cabins said to have been used by Theodore Roosevelt for hunting and fishing.

8. OLD HOMESTEAD SITE. Near Skinner Creek, the high tide trail leads past the remains of two homesteads. Rusting metal from a stove and other implements, bottles, and the mark of an old foundation can be seen.

9. SKINNER CREEK (Wabetso, meaning "little river," or tsēɫtsɛqā-la'lis (tsiɫtsakalalis), meaning "red or capberry beaches"). Near the mouth of Skinner Creek is a First Nations place of origin or an old village site (as listed by Boas).

10. SHUSHARTIE BAY (ʒuʼʒadi, pron. *Zu-zadee*, meaning "cockle bay" or "a place possessing cockles." Also, Khatis, meaning "where our forefathers lived many years ago"). The name Shushartie is an anglicized version of the First Nations name. The estuarine bay possesses an extensive tidal flat, where shellfish are prolific. There was a permanent First Nations village at the head of Shushartie Bay called Khatis. This was an important spot for fall fishing on the river, and clams and crabs were gathered here. From 1800–1836, a fur trading post operated on the west side of Shushartie Bay. Later, white settlers established the area in 1893. Robert Hunt purchased the first block of land and within 10 years, there was a small store, hotel, post office, and wharf here. In 1913, the Goletas Fish Company established a cannery. During World War II, Shushartie Bay was a staging post for goods being shipped to the Cape Scott radar base and to the few remaining settlers. On the eastern side of the bay are the graves of two seamen: Edward (surname not legible), native of Jersey City, of the ship *Maine,* of Fairhaven, died in a boat, March 1844, in the chase of a whale (a Native from Hope Island said that he died from breaking a blood vessel from overexertion); and John Thompson, seaman, native of St. Helena, died May 1844.

11. HOPE ISLAND (X̱wa̱mdasbe, pron. *Humdaspe,* meaning "place where there is otter.). A seasonal village site that later became the principal village of the combined Nahwitti tribes in the second half of the 19th century. In 1879, agent general Gilbert Sproat made a provisional allotment covering all of Hope Island as an Indian Reserve. Formerly called Valdes (after the Spanish explorer) and later renamed after an English vice-admiral.

12. BULL HARBOUR (Geya, meaning "rock across the passage"). Located on Hope Island, this is the village of the Tłatłasikwala First Nation. Named after J.A. Bull, ship's master with Captain George Richards on his 1859–65 survey of Vancouver Island.

NOT PICTURED

1. NIGEI ISLAND (ōgŭmᵉla, pron. *u'gam'la*, meaning "front rock"). Nigei was the hereditary name of the principal chief of the Nahwitti tribe (formerly Galiano Island, as named by the Spanish explorer Galiano when he and Valdes passed here in 1792).

2. SCOTT ISLANDS. Five islands make up the Scott Islands archipelago. Lanz and Cox Islands are closest to Vancouver Island and were designated as a Class "A" Provincial Park in 1995. The outer three islands of Sartine, Beresford, and Triangle (also called Anne Vallée in honour of the late biologist who died here) became provincial ecological reserves in 1971. The Scott Islands support the highest concentration of breeding seabirds in Canada's Pacific Ocean. About 40 percent of the seabirds that breed in British Columbia nest here. See page page 176 for more on the First Nations history of the Scott Islands.

KWAKWAK̲A̲'WAKW TRIBES

NAHWITTI. Through the history of the North Island, the word "Nahwitti" has referred to many things. Originally it was the name of a Tłatłasik̲wala chief and of the First Nations village at Cape Sutil. Later, the name was used to refer to the entire tribe (formerly three distinct tribes, the Tłatłasik̲wala, Nakomgilisala and Yutlinuk), as well as their village, and later Hope Island. Nahwitti was also the name of a trading centre established at Shushartie Bay. The Nahwitti Indian Reserve was established in 1886 at Cape Sutil and was once occupied with four houses and gardens.

175

Today, a variety of landscape features bear the name: Nahwitti River, Nahwitti Bar, Nahwitti Cone, and Nahwitti Plateau.

NAKAMGILISALA. Means "those of the unprotected bay" or "always staying in their country." A Kwakwaḵa'wakw tribe located at Cape Scott. Circa 1775, the Nakamgilisala's tribal territory extended from east of Cape Sutil to the Cape Scott area. According to Chief Wallas, those who moved to Quatsino Sound took on their present names, while those remaining became known by a name that means "always stay in the same place."

TŁATŁASIḴWAḺA. Means "outside, on the ocean shore" or "those of the ocean side." A Kwakwaḵa'wakw tribe located at Cape Scott. Circa 1775, the Tłatłasiḵwala's tribal territory extended from the northwest side from Shushartie Bay to just east of Cape Sutil (including Hope and Nigei Islands). Today, a small population lives in a village at Bull Harbour on Hope Island.

YUTLINUK (pron. *yut'linuxw*). Means "people of Triangle Islands." A Kwakwaḵa'wakw tribe that was located on the Scott Islands. Circa 1775, the Yutlinuk inhabited Cox and Lanz Islands. Their main village was located on Lanz Island (gʻōxdɛᵋms, pron. *gukwdams*, meaning "house site on ground"), but also lived on Triangle Island (wədi', pron. *Wadi*, meaning "where the spring is—never goes dry") and Cox Island (yut'łi). The islands were an important source of seabird eggs. These people faced harsh environmental conditions and raids—their population suffered severely and the remaining tribe joined the Nakamgilisala by mid-19th century.

PLANTS AND ANIMALS
OF THE NORTH COAST

NORTH VANCOUVER ISLAND IS alive. You'll notice this life staring you in the face the moment you arrive in Port Hardy and observe eagles, ravens, and herons hanging out in the harbour. In conversation with the water taxi captain or the shuttle bus driver, you will soon find that wildlife sightings and encounters are the common local storyline.

Within the park, the mosaic of terrestrial and marine environments creates a haven for flora and fauna: towering trees, fungi, underbrush, mosses, insects, intertidal invertebrates, birds, small mammals, amphibians, and larger mammals are to be found. It is impossible to fully describe the variety of wildlife and plants that abound. Instead, the following provides a high-level overview. Where possible, the significance of plants and animals to the Kwakwa̱ka̱'wakw is also described.

ECOSYSTEM

CAPE SCOTT PROVINCIAL PARK is considered part of the Coastal Western Hemlock biogeoclimatic zone, one of Canada's wettest ecosystems that stretches along British Columbia's coast, between the Coastal Mountains and the Pacific Ocean. A true

Human and wildlife habitat intersect on the North Island. California sea lions bask on a raft in Port Hardy. *Photo: Steve Fines*

rainforest, this zone is dominated by coniferous trees and temperate climates. Humus and nutrient-rich soils support a highly diverse and productive region. Wet ocean winds cool the landscape and influence the forest landscape. Intertidal zones create unique habitats for adapted species, and many of the plants and animals that live on the edge of this coastal landscape are reliant on the marine environment's bountiful food sources.

AS YOU HIKE THROUGH the park you will notice how the plant and animal life changes dramatically depending on the elevation, sun, wind exposure, topography, moisture, and proximity to the coast.

Eagles feasting on snapper and salmon. *Photo: Steve Fines*

It is surprising how areas of the park can differ so dramatically. Try to observe some of the complex interrelationships—how seedlings spring up from a fallen tree, how gaps in the forest canopy encourage a different kind of undergrowth, or how, as you near the beaches, the vegetation and birdsong changes.

VEGETATION

WITHIN CAPE SCOTT PROVINCIAL Park, mixed forests create important multi-layered habitats. Standing dead trees, "snags," are important for nesting and insect foraging. Where trees have fallen, increased sunlight prompts the growth of other types of plants. Fallen and decomposing trees act as nurse logs for young saplings to grow. When they fall into streams, large logs create pools and influence stream ecology.

The most common tree species of this region are western hemlock, western red cedar and Sitka spruce. Douglas fir and yellow cedar are also present. North Vancouver Island is considered to have some of the world's best growth of these species, so it is not surprising that forestry has been such a mainstay of the region's economy. A quick look at satellite imagery from Google Earth will reveal an extensive patchwork of logging activity.

Sitka spruce occurs commonly along the coastlines and floodplains, thriving in areas with well-drained soil and tolerating salt-water spray from the ocean. Yellow cedar and lodgepole pine are common in the upland bog areas.

Old-growth trees (those over 250 years old) can be found through the park and are most visible as you head inland. Old-growth spruce forest is particularly prominent in the Strandby River valley, and the valley around Shushartie Bay. In areas that have been logged (such as around the Nahwitti River), you will likely see early-colonizing trees such as the deciduous red alder.

MAJOR TREES IN CAPE SCOTT PROVINCIAL PARK

WESTERN HEMLOCK: drooping crowns with graceful boughs, flat small needles, and relatively smooth bark. Shade tolerant; grows beneath other species.

SITKA SPRUCE: has scaly bark and very sharp needles. Tolerant of salt water and found close to the shoreline.

WESTERN RED CEDAR: ropy reddish-brown bark. Important in First Nations culture and the official tree of BC. Leaves are lighter green than yellow cedar.

YELLOW CEDAR: greyish brown bark, drooping, vertically hanging branches, somewhat flattened; bluish-green leaves partly overlapping in a shingled arrangement.

DOUGLAS FIR: generally found in younger, more open forests. Thick, ridged bark. Cones have three-pronged bracts.

LODEPOLE PINE: branches are stout; sharp, long needles in twos, deep green to yellowish-green.

You may notice that the tops of many of the red and yellow cedar are dead, their naked spikes poking amongst the green canopy. This occurs because cedars require lots of calcium, particularly for the development of their tops. Significant rainfall and river flow causes a leaching of valuable nutrients. Biologists think that the spiked tops have been caused by calcium deficiencies in the moist, acidic soils of these areas.

Trees were invaluable to the culture and livelihood of the First Nations, who traditionally used them for building longhouses and totem poles, creating art and tools, and constructing canoes. Roots were used to make baskets, and bark was woven into rope, nets, clothing, and halibut line. Branches were soaked in urine to soften the fibres and make them rot-resistant before

A young sword fern. *Photo: Andrew Bruce Lau*

use in lashing and sewing. Yellow cedar was prized for clothing, and carved into many things from paddles to totems. Red cedar is considered so vital to the culture and livelihood of the Kwakwaka'wakw that it is called the "tree of life." Between Cape Sutil and Shuttleworth Bight keep your eyes out for signs of culturally modified trees (see page 64 for details).

UNDERSTORY

Ocean mist is a dominant influence on understory plants, particularly near beaches. Common understory plants include lily of the valley and bedstraw. Nearest to the forest edge will be salal, salmonberry, huckleberry, Oregon grape, and grasses. Common throughout are lichen, fungi, skunk cabbage, and ferns including licorice fern, deer fern, bracken fern, and sword fern. Where hemlock grows, you will notice little understory—the needles that fall are so acidic they prohibit new growth of other species. Mosses are abundant in this ecosystem and there are several species including sphagnum moss, step moss, and lanky moss throughout the area.

UPLAND BOGS

Cape Scott Provincial Park protects part of a unique ecosystem of upland bogs. These extensive peatland areas are located on elevated plateaus and are characterized by stagnant marshy

Sphagnum moss, young salal and deer fern.

181

Marshy tributaries of the upland bog ecosystem.

areas, muskeg ground cover, and sparse, scrub forest (often the result of acidic environment caused by poor drainage). Lodgepole pine and yellow cedar are common in these environments. The plateau is a mix of open meadows, patches of forested areas, small ponds, waterways, and swamps.

The upland bog between the Nahwitti and Strandby Rivers is one of the largest intact coastal wetlands in British Columbia. You will glimpse this as you pass between Shushartie Bay and Skinner Creek. The bog landscape provides important nesting habitat for sandhill cranes, as well as a home to a variety of endemic species. The firm mounds of moss that form in this poorly drained terrain are likely peat mosses such as *Sphagnum austinii* (tough peat moss).

COASTAL HEADLANDS AND BEACHES

Beaches and intertidal zones present unique environments for life to adapt. Vegetation that is found in beach areas includes small herbs and grasses, berries, seabeach sandwort, hairy rockcress, Indian paintbrush, sea plantain, beach pea, and sea milkwort. On the more exposed rocky headlands you will find

Sand dunes near Guise Bay.

hardy plants such as rusty saxifrage, western yew and saskatoon berry. Within the marine environment are a variety of seaweeds, including rockweed and bull kelp.

The sand dunes near Guise Bay are one of the most unique features in the park. Here, native plants include arrow grass, sedges, and coast strawberry. A variety of non-native species also grow here—introduced when these dunes were farmed. Some of these plants include hyacinth, daffodils, holly, ivy, laurel, rhododendron, monkey-puzzle trees, and cinquefoil.

WILDLIFE

THE COASTAL WESTERN HEMLOCK Zone encompasses one of the most diverse and abundant wildlife habitats in all of BC. Within Cape Scott Provincial Park, you will encounter a variety of animals that have populated this region for thousands of years. They are integral to the landscape and part of the unique fabric of this place. The following provides an overview of some of the animals living here, as well as some highlight species.

Black bears are prevalent on the North Island. Here, a mother bear and her two cubs forage the beach in search of food.
Photo: Steve Fines

MAMMALS

In the forest or on the beach, you may spot a variety of mammals such as black bear, wolves, cougars, Roosevelt elk, and black tailed deer. Closer observation will allow you to spot smaller wildlife such as squirrels and mink.

Out in the ocean or at its periphery, you may see other kinds of mammals, such as sea otters, harbour seals, and sea lions. Whales are also found along this coast—both orcas (also known as killer whales) and gray whales are frequently sighted feeding amongst the kelp beds. If you are lucky you will spot them or enormous humpback whales. Porpoises also make their home here, feeding on salmon, trout, and other fishes.

Wolf at Shushartie Bay.
Photo: Graham Smith

Wolves are usually elusive but you will likely see their tracks on the beach or hear their howls at night. The Vancouver Island wolf, a subspecies of grey wolf, is endemic to the island. At Cape Scott, there is a healthy population. Wolves usually roam in packs of 7 or 8 animals, preying on deer and elk. They are also opportunistic feeders who will eat salmon, intertidal organisms, seals, river otters, or anything tasty the tide presents on the beach. Habitat fragmentation and destruction, which affects them and their prey, is their main threat. The total population on Vancouver Island is estimated to be several hundred.

At the top of the marine food chain is the orca (also known as the killer whale or blackfish). This is one of the most iconic species of the Pacific Northwest. Orcas are known to live in the same group or pod of up to 40 individuals their entire lives. Their communication and hunting behaviours are unique to a particular group and passed from generation to generation. Orcas are the largest members of the dolphin family and are powerful predators with hunting techniques that have often been compared to that of wolf packs. Resident populations stay near to shore, do not migrate, and eat mainly salmon, herring, and other small fish. Transient populations have a broader habitat range and hunt larger marine mammals, such as seals, sea lions, dolphins, and other whales as well as fish.

Orcas (max'inux") are frequently mentioned in First Nations oral history, and are featured in traditional designs and in ceremonial activities. They are thought to have the power to drive away illness—if a sick person saw an orca near the beach, they would go to the water, take a mouthful of water and blow it towards the whale addressing it as "Long-Life Maker."

Would you guess that the cuddly-looking sea otter is a member of the weasel family? Perhaps harder to imagine is how this animal narrowly avoided extinction when European traders discovered its soft, thick pelt. Extirpated from Vancouver Island by the early 1900s, a reintroduction of 89 individuals in 1969 has grown today to an estimated 3,000 living from Cape Scott to the west coast of the island. Sea otters live mostly on the water and their primary habitat is kelp beds. Their coat is thicker than any other mammal at about 165,000 hairs per square centimetre, providing essential insulation from the cold water. The sea otter eats bottom-dwelling invertebrates and shellfish including sea urchins, clams, mussels, and crabs, as well as fish. They are often seen smashing open shells with rocks while floating on their backs. Sea otters are considered a keystone species, meaning they have an effect on the ecosystem that is greater in proportion to the numbers of otters living in the community. Its control of the sea urchin population is the sole reason the urchins do not decimate the kelp forests. When the otters were hunted to near extinction, the kelp forests and the vast majority of the life living in them, vanished. With the reintroduction of sea otters, urchin populations are kept in check, and the kelp forests are coming back.

BIRDS

Birds are prolific in the forest and in the marine environment of the north coast. Along the shore and in estuaries you will see a variety of waterfowl such as bufflehead, common goldeneye, black oystercatcher, harlequin duck, surf scoter, common merganser, and many species of gulls. The nutrient-rich, protected waters of estuaries and tidal flat ecosystems are prime feeding grounds for a variety of shore and migratory birds. Trumpeter swans, grebes, scoters, great blue herons, Canada geese, sandhill cranes and common snipe are often found at the head of Hansen Lagoon. Spotted sandpiper, semipalmated plover, and killdeer are frequently seen feeding in flocks on the mud flats.

The Cape Scott region is part of the Pacific Flyway, a major north-south travel route for migratory birds in the Americas, extending all the way from the Arctic Circle, down the Pacific Coast to Patagonia. Every year, migratory birds travel some or all of this distance, both in spring and in fall, following food sources, and travelling to breeding grounds and overwintering sites.

The forest attracts birds that prefer its shelter, nesting habitat, or the presence of food (other birds, rodents, bark and wood-boring insects, seeds, and berries). In the forest you may see hummingbirds, owls, woodpeckers, crows, ravens, Steller's jays, warblers, and finches (chestnut-backed chickadee, red-breasted nuthatch, winter wren, and varied thrush, among others).

The Scott Islands are also notable for bird life. This string of five islands lies 10 to 46 km (around 6 to 29 mi) off the northwest tip of Vancouver Island and provides the most important breeding grounds for seabirds in British Columbia. Lanz and Cox Islands are closest of the islands to Vancouver Island and were designated as a Class "A" Provincial Park in 1995. The outer three islands of Sartine, Beresford, and Triangle (Anne Vallée) became provincial Ecological Reserves in 1971. These outer three islands support over 2 million breeding birds, about 40 percent of BC's

Harlequin duck (male).
Photo: Graham Smith

Bald eagle. *Photo: Graham Smith*

breeding seabird population. Colonies of auklets, puffins, common murres, cormorants, and gulls find sanctuary in this isolated environment. They house 90 percent of the tufted puffins in Canada and approximately half of all Cassin's auklets in the world. The Scott Islands marine area is internationally recognized and one of the most ecologically vital locations in the Northwest Pacific Ocean ecosystem.

On the coast, bald eagles soar through the skies or watch with still intensity from snags high above. They are Canada's largest bird of prey, and can have a wingspan over 2 m (around 6.6 ft) long. The head and tail are white and the body dark brown. Juveniles are entirely brown. This animal is built to hunt and scavenge—it has a giant yellow beak and talons. Small spikes (spicules) on its feet allow it to grasp prey like slippery fish. Eagles can see 4–7 times farther than a human. Cape Scott provides year-round habitat for eagles, providing easy access to fish. Bald eagles mate for life and use the same nest, adding to it every year. You will see many of these enormous nests along the coastline, particularly on the stretch from Nahwitti River to Shushartie Bay.

The tail feathers of bald eagles ("kwikw" in Kwak'wala) were regularly used in First Nations ceremonies, including the ceremonies for curing the sick. Eagle down was used during the performance of the Tła'sala or peace dance. In ancient times, if two chiefs fought, they would dance the Tła'sala dance together. As the eagle down from within their headdresses settled to the floor, so too would their anger towards one another. The eagle is a family crest figure and is frequently depicted in First Nations designs.

Ravens are intelligent, opportunistic, and curious. Mostly living alone or in pairs, ravens are playful, graceful, and highly observant. Who knows what secret joke ravens enjoy as they chortle through the woods, or what magic they stir with their croaks. Ravens have an omnivorous diet that includes small animals, insects, and fruits. They are about twice the size of the average crow and have black iridescent feathers.

For the Kwakwaka'wakw, ravens (gwa'wina) are thought to have supernatural powers and to know many things. They were believed to never die of sickness, so their skin was often placed under the head or on the chest of a sickly infant to improve its condition. The variety of calls are said to have many different meanings or predictions such as war, sickness, death, weather forecasts, and the arrival of strangers.

REPTILES AND AMPHIBIANS

The damp environment of the north coast supports a healthy amphibian population. Species such as the western red-backed salamander, red-legged frog, Pacific tree frog and the western toad dwell on the forest floor, in bogs, and in wetland and riparian areas. In drier, warmer areas you are likely to stumble upon the common garter snake basking in the sun.

FISH

The North Island region supports a wide variety of fish, from purely oceanic species (such as rockfish, sole, Pacific herring, Pacific halibut and spiny dogfish), to fish that spawn in fresh water but live as adults in marine waters (such as salmon, coastal cutthroat trout, and eulachon), to species that exclusively live in freshwater lakes and creeks (such as sculpins). The rivers and estuaries within Cape Scott provide habitat for a wide array of fish. Highly valued river systems—particularly the Strandby and Shushartie Rivers—provide spawning and rearing habitat for salmon, namely sockeye, coho, pink, chum, and steelhead. Due to past logging activities, the Nahwitti River is not in such pristine condition, but also contains salmon, as well as Dolly Varden trout and sculpin. Cutthroat trout and salmon can also be found in Hansen Lagoon, Fisherman River, and Eric Lake.

Mature salmon make their way from the rivers to the Pacific Ocean. The Pacific fish species are too numerous to list in detail. Migratory species, such as salmon, herring, and eulachon provide seasonal feasting opportunities for seals, sea lions, gulls, bald eagles, bears, and people. In the past, the Kwakwa̱ka̱'wakw would journey to Knight Inlet (Dzawadi) to follow the age-old tradition of rendering t'lina, the oil of the eulachon fish. Eulachon is a silvery smelt sometimes called candlefish because of its high fat content that allows it to be burned as a candle. T'lina is a food staple, a condiment, a highly prized medicine,

Red-backed salamander. *Photo: Graham Smith*

Green shore crab. *Photo: Graham Smith*

and holds great importance in potlatches as a symbol of cultural wealth for Native people all along the west coast. Eulachon trading routes were once known as grease trails.

MOLLUSKS, CRUSTACEANS, AND SEA URCHINS

A whole different world exists in the marine environment. Life is uniquely adapted to the ever-changing intertidal zones and the saline ocean environment. Crabs, mollusks (clams and their relatives), and other invertebrates, cling to the shores and rocky cliff edges, or take shelter in the forests of seaweed and algae. You may see crabs, sea stars, chiton, abalone, mussels, clams, acorn barnacles, or urchins.

REGIONAL INFORMATION

NORTH ISLAND COMMUNITIES AND OTHER THINGS TO SEE AND DO

THE NORTH ISLAND FEELS different from even the small cities elsewhere on Vancouver Island. It's not just the absence of urban bustle or the whittled-down human population. The forest closes in around the grey ribbon of lonely highway as you head north and you feel nature all around. From windswept bluffs, through lush forests, to the pounding surf along the jagged coast, this region has more than a few jewels to discover.

NORTH ISLAND COMMUNITIES

THE NORTH ISLAND REGION is approximately half of Vancouver Island, yet its population is only about 2 percent of the total for Vancouver Island. Within its regional boundaries, the human population numbers approximately 12,000. The largest communities in the North Island region are Port Hardy (pop. 4,000), Port McNeill (pop. 2,600), and Cormorant Island (pop. 1,300).

The economies of these communities are primarily resource-based—fishing, logging, and mining have been the pillars of the North Island economy for over 100 years. The region is among Canada's largest timber producers, and commercial fishing and aquaculture are also major industries. The local reliance on resources is shifting to include a growing tourism sector, particularly eco-tourism.

HOLBERG

You will travel past the tiny village of Holberg on your way in or out from the San Josef/Cape Scott trailhead of Cape Scott Provincial Park. Nestled at the west end of Holberg Inlet, the village was named after a Danish historian and writer by the Danish settlers who came here in 1895. Their farms and homesteads peppered the region. When the logging industry boomed, Holberg became the site of the world's largest floating logging camp. It was later the site of a Canadian Air Force radar station. Access to this community is via a 50-km (around 31-mi) gravel logging road leading west from Port Hardy.

PORT HARDY

Highway 19 terminates at Port Hardy. With 4,000 people, this is the largest community of the North Island region. The town is tucked along the shores of Hardy Bay. Port Hardy is the gateway to Cape Scott Provincial Park—both the shuttle and the water taxi depart from here. A BC Ferries terminal is also located here for those looking to head north up BC's coast. The town has a good range of restaurants, services, and accommodations.

COAL HARBOUR

Coal Harbour is named after a small (and unsuccessful) local coal mine founded in 1883. At one time, the village was a busy whaling station. It operated until population decline and international conservation pacts closed the station in 1967. There is a 6-m (around 20-ft) blue whale jawbone on display in the town. Today, Coal Harbour offers seaplane services and connections to major fishing lodges. There is a general store and a local government wharf. Nearby is the headquarters and main community of the Quatsino First Nation.

QUATSINO

Located on Quatsino Sound, the hamlet of Quatsino is a 20-minute water taxi ride from Coal Harbour. It was settled by Norwegians in search of their own utopia in 1894. Today, the population is about 75. The one-room schoolhouse is still used, and there is a post office and a few accommodation services.

WINTER HARBOUR

If you continue on the gravel road west from Holberg, you reach the edge of the Pacific Ocean and the outpost community of Winter Harbour. The rustic village has offered shelter for sailing ships and fishing vessels for over a century. Today, it is known for its saltwater fishing charters and is the only stationary fuelling facility in Quatsino Sound.

PORT MCNEILL

Home to the world's largest burl (weighing 24 tonnes and about 525 years old!), Port McNeill was once a base camp for loggers. Keeping the burl company are about 2,600 residents. The town remains a hub for forestry—two million hectares of forested land are administered out of Port McNeill, supplying 8 percent of the total provincial harvest. This town is a departure point for Sointula and Alert Bay. Kayakers, scuba divers, and boaters destined for the Broughton Archipelago also depart from here. The seawall is a great place to take a walk, and it leads you to the School House Creek Trail.

SOINTULA

Meaning "place of harmony" in Finnish, Sointula is located on Malcolm Island, a 25-minute sailing from Port McNeill. This town was established by Scandinavian immigrants in 1901. Their vision of a utopian socialist community failed, but a population of about 800 continues to live on the island. The museum provides more detail about the interesting history and there is an eclectic artistic presence. There are free bicycles available to explore the island. The 3-km (just under 2-mi) Meteoja Heritage Trail is accessible from town, and the Beautiful Bay Trail and Bere Point Regional Park are also worth exploring. Sointula is home to BC's oldest cooperative store, as well as several other cooperative enterprises.

ALERT BAY

Located on Cormorant Island (a 20-minute ferry ride from Port McNeill), Alert Bay was the traditional summer village for the 'Namgis First Nation before European settlers arrived in the 1860s. It was established as a salmon fishing port and regional trading centre. Today the 'Namgis people welcome visitors to respectfully explore backyard treasures like the tribal Big House, the world's tallest totem pole, and the U'mista Cultural Centre, which showcases a unique potlatch collection. A network of nature trails and boardwalk leads you through the ecological reserve to marshes, rainforests, and culturally modified trees. There is an oceanfront boardwalk, accommodation, galleries, gift shops, and diners at Alert Bay.

PORT ALICE

Located on a mountainside facing Neroutsos Inlet, Port Alice (pop. 800) is known for its coastal beauty, fishing, and its pulp mill. Hiking and caving are nearby and mountain biking is popular. The town hosts the annual Rumble Fest, part of the Island Cup mountain biking series.

TELEGRAPH COVE

Over a century ago, this tiny community was nothing more than the most-northern station of the Campbell River telegraph line. Settlers, loggers, and fishermen would come here to connect with the outside world. Today, the waterfront boardwalk community is an eco-tourism destination. Located on Johnstone

Strait and close to Robson Bight, Telegraph Cove is renowned as a whale-watching destination.

SAYWARD

The oceanside village of Sayward is the first town north of Campbell River. Home to about 400 people, Sayward also attracts its share of visitors. Adjacent to the Robson Bight Ecological Reserve, whale and wildlife watching is common (you can also try listening for them from the hydrophone at the Port of Kelsey Bay wharf). Nature lovers will also like to walk beneath the giant Douglas firs at White River Park, attempt the Kusam Klimb hike up Mount H'Kusam, or birdwatch at the Salmon River Wildlife Reserve.

WOSS (AND THE NIMPKISH VALLEY)

If you've heard of Woss it is likely in conjunction with Mount Cain, a community-owned and -operated ski hill with a reputation for powder without the crowds. Woss and the surrounding Nimpkish Valley is home to just over 200 people. The town is located along a historical First Nations trade route that linked the east and west coasts of north Vancouver Island. More recently, the Nimpkish Valley was a logging town, connected to the rest of the world by the longest working railway in North America.

ZEBALLOS

The quiet port community of Zeballos (pop. 230) was active gold-rush territory circa World War II. Surrounded by mountains, forests, and coastline, Zeballos is an outdoor recreation destination (fishing, kayaking, hiking, rock climbing, caving, and diving are all available). It is remote—a 2.5-hour drive north from Campbell River, including the last 40 km (around 35 mi) on gravel logging roads. Zeballos is often used as a gateway to more adventures in the area: Kyuquot Sound, the Brooks Peninsula, and Nootka Sound are all accessible from here.

OTHER PROVINCIAL PARKS

RAFT COVE PROVINCIAL PARK is a beautiful destination for day hikers, overnight campers, and surfers. The park is walk-in only. Hiking from the parking lot to the beach takes about 45 minutes and the trail emerges at a beautiful sandy beach with few people. Access to the park is via the Ronning Main logging road (about 1.5 hours' drive from Port Hardy).

QUATSINO PROVINCIAL PARK is located on the north side of Quatsino Sound, southeast of Holberg. The park is marine-access only and there are no established campsites or maintained trails. It is possible to camp at the estuary or beach. This undeveloped park protects some of the largest old-growth trees along Quatsino's coastline. Situated along the popular Quatsino Sound kayak touring route, this park can be used by visitors as an overnight stopover or as a scenic place to enjoy a picnic.

MARBLE RIVER PROVINCIAL PARK is about a 30-minute drive from Port Hardy. The hiking and biking trail is 4.2 km (around 2.6 mi) one way, beneath a stunning rainforest canopy with views of the Marble River. This is a great place to watch the salmon spawn in the fall. Camping is allowed here and at a forest recreation site adjacent to the park. The Marble River is considered one of the best steelhead fishing rivers on Vancouver Island.

NIMPKISH LAKE PROVINCIAL PARK is located in the Tlakwa Creek watershed, 32 km (around 20 mi) south of Port McNeill at the south end of Nimpkish Lake. This wilderness park is popular with windsurfers and those looking for a remote camping destination. Visitors are surrounded by beautiful views of the Karmutzen mountain range and old-growth hemlock. Fishing and canoeing are possible on the lake.

OUTDOOR RECREATION:
TOP 10 NORTH ISLAND ACTIVITIES (ASIDE FROM VISITING CAPE SCOTT PROVINCIAL PARK)

1. SKIING AT MOUNT CAIN. Mount Cain is known for the best powder skiing on Vancouver Island and was voted one of the best community ski hills in Canada by *Ski Canada Magazine*. The ski season runs weekends from December to April (with the exception of Christmas and spring break).

2. CAVING. Vancouver Island has over 1,000 caves. According to the Vancouver Island Cave Exploration Group, there are more explored limestone caves here than in all other Canadian provinces combined! The North Island is famous for karst, unusual land formations, and a high concentration of caves. Significant rainfall, thick vegetation, soil cover and steep terrain all contribute to the well-developed caves—many of them concentrated in the Quatsino Formation. Many of the caves in the region are located in difficult terrain and should only be visited by experienced cavers or with guides.

   At Little Huson Cave Regional Park, near Woss, find large limestone features, karst rock arches, and deep pools filled with clear green water from Little Huson Lake.

KARST is a kind of topography in which the landscape is largely shaped by the dissolving action of water on carbonate bedrock. Caused by a geological process occurring over thousands of years, it results in unusual surface and sub-surface features including sinkholes, springs, vertical shafts, disappearing streams, and complex underground drainage systems.

From Port Alice, visit the Devil's Bath (a sinkhole filled with water from an underground stream), the Eternal Fountain (a cave with passages sculpted from red rock), and Disappearing River. These rare limestone formations are part of the extensive karst system of the region.

3. DIVING in the cold waters off the coast of North Vancouver Island is renowned, with great visibility and a diversity of marine species including Pacific white-sided dolphins, wolf eels, octopuses, anemones, and sponges. Topping the list of favourite and famous sites are the Browning Wall, God's Pocket Provincial Park, Five Fathom Rock, Seven Tree Island, and Hunt Rock.

4. SURFING the unpopulated waves on the northwest coast is increasing in popularity at destinations like Raft Cove, Grant Bay, and San Josef Bay. Surfboard and wetsuit rentals are available in Port Hardy. Windsurfing and kiteboarding on windy Nimpkish Lake is considered world class and the coast near Port McNeill is also known to be good. Paddle boarding is available in the Nimpkish Valley.

5. KAYAKING. A combination of incredible landscape scenery, protected waters, and unbeatable wildlife-viewing opportunities make ocean kayaking a must-do on the North Island. The Lonely Planet travel guide ranked whale watching from a kayak in Johnstone Strait number two in their Top 10 list of Canadian Adventures. A variety of tour operators offer rentals, day tours, and lessons, as well as multi-day adventures. For adrenaline seekers, white-water rafting is available in the Nimpkish Valley.

6. MOUNTAIN BIKING. A combination of logging roads, single track, and double track make the North Island a fantastic mountain biking destination for all abilities. Some key locations include

Rumble Mountain Bike Trail (and annual Rumble Fest race) near Port Alice, Sayward, Woss/Nimpkish Valley (including Mount Cain), Port McNeill, and the Echo Lake system near Port Hardy. The best way to find trails is to talk to the locals. A couple of good starting points are North Star Cycle and Sports in Port Hardy and The Shed Outdoor Store in Port McNeill.

7. HIKING. There are endless hiking opportunities of varying lengths on the North Island. The following is just a small sampling:

- MOUNT H'KUSAM (Sayward). Not for the weak-of-heart, this rugged 23-km (14.3-mi) loop goes up and over Mount H'Kusam and down the Stowe Creek watershed. The challenge and the scenery of the route have inspired the annual Kusam Klimb trail race in June.

- MARBLE RIVER PROVINCIAL PARK (near Port Alice). An 8.4-km (around 5.2-mi) return trip (out and back) through beautiful rainforest. Average hiking time one way: 1.5 hours.

- TEX LYON TRAIL (Port Hardy). A challenging hike that starts at the harbour and takes you to Dillon Point, providing views of the Queen Charlotte Strait and Fort Rupert. Watch for tides and allow a minimum 8 hours for the round trip.

- QUATSE RIVER AND ESTUARY TRAILS (Port Hardy). This pretty trail and great birdwatching destination meanders along the waterfront from the seaplane base before splitting into the estuary trail and the Quatse River Loop. Access the end of Hardy Bay and the Quatse River estuary by taking the road to the BC Ferries terminal from Highway 19. Turn left onto Goodspeed Road, a gravel road, and continue to the end of Hardy Bay.

- ALERT BAY (Cormorant Island). An impressive 16-km (just under 10-mi) trail network extends around the island and includes the Alert Bay Ecological Reserve (also known as Gator Gardens), where a boardwalk stroll features culturally modified trees.

8. WILDLIFE WATCHING doesn't get much better than on north Vancouver Island. On land, you may see black bears, wolves, deer, elk, and cougar. At sea, humpback whales, dolphins, seals, sea lions, orcas, and countless seabirds.
   - BEAR WATCHING. The prime time to spot black bears is from spring mating season (May) to fall salmon runs (October). Knight Inlet and the Great Bear Rainforest area are considered two of the best places to view bears, wolves, and bald eagles.
   - WHALE WATCHING. Salmon migrations and rubbing beaches at Robson Bight Ecological Reserve attract many orcas to the region. The best time to go is between late June and early October. Many local communities offer whale-watching tours.

9. BEACH WALKING. Explore intertidal life, stroll along sandy shores, or have a relaxing picnic. The following are some of the best beaches of the region, many requiring travel along logging roads:
   - STOREY'S BEACH. A 12-minute drive from downtown Port Hardy, this beach is particularly beautiful at low tide.
   - RAFT COVE. Within Raft Cove Provincial Park at the mouth of the Macjack River. Access is by a gravel logging road out of Holberg and a 2-km (1.2-mi) trail from the parking lot.
   - CAPE PALMERSTON. Located north of Raft Cove by logging road. An emergency cabin and a few rustic campsites are available here.
   - GRANT BAY. From Holberg drive south and turn right at West Main junction before you reach Winter Harbour. Follow the posted signs to the trailhead. Find nearly 1 km (0.6 mi) of sandy beach on the north entrance to Quatsino Sound.
   - BERE POINT PARK. Located on Malcolm Island's north, this beautiful beach is also a known rubbing beach for whales. The Beautiful Bay Trail begins at the Bere Point campground.

10. FISHING. Healthy rivers and lakes, tidal inlets, and the Pacific Ocean provide fabulous year-round freshwater and saltwater fishing. Saltwater fishing includes salmon, halibut, crab, rockfish, sea bass, and snapper (peak season for saltwater fishing runs from May to early October). Many charters are available. Freshwater anglers can choose from dozens of lakes and rivers. Marble River Provincial Park is a very popular destination for recreational angling and is considered to be one of the best steelhead fishing rivers on Vancouver Island. The most popular fly-fishing location, known as the Emerald Pool, is located at the end of the 4.2-km (2.6-mi) Marble River Trail.

CULTURAL AND HISTORICAL ATTRACTIONS

U'MISTA CULTURAL CENTRE (Alert Bay, Cormorant Island). Working to ensure the survival of all aspects of cultural heritage of the Kwakwaka'wakw, the U'mista Cultural Centre has a world-famous collection of items related to potlatch ceremonies, as well as several other exhibits about the ethnobiology of the Kwakwaka'wakw. There are also displays of historical and contemporary Kwakwaka'wakw objects. Cultural storytelling and traditional dances occur in the summer. See page 153 for more information.

FORT RUPERT. Once the site of a Hudson's Bay Company fort, this Kwakiutl (Kwagu'ł) village has several historic and cultural sites of interest, including a Big House built for ceremonial purposes, a historical cemetery, totem poles, a church, and the first corner store on the North Island. An old chimney marks the site of the fort, built in 1849. Visit the Copper Maker Gallery to see master carvers such as Calvin Hunt at work.

Totems standing watch outside the U'mista Cultural Centre, Cormorant Island.

TOTEM POLES. Throughout the north Vancouver Island region are many elaborately carved totem poles, including the world's tallest in Alert Bay. Totem poles are located around the region including at Fort Rupert Reserve, Bear Cove ferry terminal, and elsewhere around Port Hardy.

SOINTULA MUSEUM. Located on Malcolm Island, this museum features interesting artifacts, publications, and photographs about the development of this community from a Finnish socialist commune to the quiet village of today.

PORT HARDY MUSEUM AND ARCHIVES. Exhibits feature aboriginal artifacts, objects left behind by early settlers, natural history materials, and local industrial equipment. The museum also hosts a temporary exhibit from April to October each year and has a variety of local book publications and arts and crafts for sale.

PORT MCNEILL HERITAGE MUSEUM. Located in a log house, this museum pays tribute to the history of the local forestry industry.

OTHER UNIQUE POINTS OF INTEREST

SHOE TREE. Past Holberg on the route to Cape Scott Provincial Park, you will pass by the Shoe Tree, an old cedar snag covered with hundreds of shoes—from hiking boots to stilettos—left by passing travellers. The sight was apparently started after a woman destroyed her shoes on the Cape Scott hike, and decided to make a tribute to the hike by nailing her shoes to a tree.

RONNING'S GARDEN. In 1910, Bernt Ronning, a Norwegian immigrant, built his homestead near Holberg. As he cleared away the dense forest, he planted around 2 ha (5 acres) with exotic seeds and cuttings from around the world. Thanks to a dedicated restoration effort to clear the years of overgrowth, the garden can now be accessed. Between Holberg and the Cape Scott/San Josef Bay trailhead parking lot, look for the wooden sign on the right of the road. A 10-minute walk on a restored section of the San Josef Wagon Road leads you to the garden.

PETROGLYPHS exist at Fort Rupert on the sandstone formations in the higher tidal zones below the old Hudson's Bay fort.

THE WHALE INTERPRETIVE CENTRE at Telegraph Cove offers a closer look at whales and many other mammal species of the Pacific Northwest. The centre has a blue whale skeleton on display.

THE QUATSE SALMON STEWARDSHIP CENTRE AND HATCHERY at Port Hardy is combined interpretive centre, salmon hatchery, aquarium, and educational facility. It features interactive exhibits, theatre, and a display of ocean creatures from around

Look for the sign leading to Bernt Ronning's amazing garden on your way to the Cape Scott trailhead.

the area. Tours, workshops, and courses on stream stewardship and habitat enhancement are also offered. There is a pond behind the hatchery that is open for fish feeding and nature trails along the river that provide visitors with information on many species of flora and fauna.

THE BC COAST. BC Ferries offers the 15-hour Inside Passage voyage between Port Hardy and Prince Rupert from mid-May to the end of September. The rest of the year, the Inside Passage operates as an overnight sailing with stops along the way (20–22 hours sailing time). The Discovery Coast Passage is a summer-only route between Port Hardy and ports on BC's mainland coast (20–33 hours sailing time from Port Hardy to Bella Coola depending on the route).

A FEW GREAT FOOD STOPS ON THE NORTH ISLAND

CAFÉ GUIDO, 7135 Market Street, Port Hardy. A great café, with tasty breakfast and lunch options, art, and a downstairs bookstore.

TOUDAI SUSHI, 7370 Market Street, Port Hardy. A good sushi restaurant with great views of Hardy Bay.

SCARLET IBIS PUB, 32 E Hardy Way. Overlooking the Holberg Inlet, this isolated pub has cold beer and burgers—well worth a stop.

HARDY BUOYS SMOKED FISH, 9300 Trustee Road. Buy smoked fish delicacies, locally caught fresh seafood, and more at this local business.

APPENDIX 1

LEAVE NO TRACE: SEVEN WAYS TO BE A MORE RESPONSIBLE HIKER

THE MEMBER-DRIVEN LEAVE NO TRACE Center for Outdoor Ethics teaches people how to enjoy the outdoors responsibly. This information has been reprinted with permission from the Leave No Trace Center for Outdoor Ethics. For more information visit www.lnt.org.

PLAN AHEAD AND PREPARE

· Know the regulations and special concerns for the area you'll visit.
· Prepare for extreme weather, hazards, and emergencies.
· Schedule your trip to avoid times of high use.
· Visit in small groups when possible. Consider splitting larger groups into smaller groups.
· Repackage food to minimize waste.
· Use a map and compass to eliminate the use of marking paint, rock cairns or flagging.

TRAVEL AND CAMP ON DURABLE SURFACES

- Durable surfaces include established trails and campsites, rock, gravel, dry grasses, and snow.
- Protect riparian areas by camping at least 60 m (200 ft) from lakes and streams.
- Good campsites are found, not made. Altering a site is usually not necessary.
- In popular areas:
    - Concentrate use on existing trails and campsites.
    - Walk single-file in the middle of the trail, even when wet or muddy.
    - Keep campsites small. Focus activity in areas where vegetation is absent.
- In pristine areas:
    - Disperse use to prevent the creation of campsites and trails.
    - Avoid places where impacts are beginning to show.

DISPOSE OF WASTE PROPERLY

- Pack it in, pack it out. Inspect your campsite and rest areas for trash or spilled foods and make sure to pack it all out.
- Deposit solid human waste in holes dug 6–8 inches deep, at least 60 m (200 ft) from water, camp, and trails. Cover the hole when finished.
- Pack out toilet paper and hygiene products.
- To wash yourself or your dishes, carry water 60 m (200 ft) away from streams or lakes and use small amounts of biodegradable soap. Scatter strained dishwater on the ground.

LEAVE WHAT YOU FIND

- Preserve the past. Examine, but do not touch cultural or historical structures and artifacts.
- Leave rocks, plants, and other natural objects as you find them.
- Avoid introducing or transporting non-native species.
- Do not build structures, furniture, or dig trenches.

MINIMIZE CAMPFIRE IMPACTS

- Campfires can cause lasting impacts to the backcountry. Use a lightweight stove for cooking and enjoy a candle lantern for light.
- Where fires are permitted, use established fire rings, fire pans, or mound fires.
- Keep fires small. Only use sticks from the ground that can be broken by hand.
- Burn all wood and coals to ash, put out campfires completely, and then scatter cool ashes.

RESPECT WILDLIFE

- Observe wildlife from a distance. Do not follow or approach animals.
- Never feed animals. Feeding wildlife damages its health, alters natural behaviours, and exposes animals to predators and other dangers.
- Protect wildlife and your food by storing rations and trash securely.
- Control pets at all times, or leave them at home.
- Avoid wildlife during sensitive times, i.e. during mating, nesting, raising young, and winter.

BE CONSIDERATE OF OTHER VISITORS

· Respect other visitors and protect the quality of their experience.
· Be courteous. Yield to other users on the trail.
· Step to the downhill side of the trail when encountering pack stock (animals that carry a load).
· Take breaks and camp away from trails and other visitors.
· Let nature's sounds prevail. Avoid loud voices and noises.

Sturdy trail construction on the North Coast Trail.

APPENDIX 2
SERVICE PROVIDERS AND OTHER USEFUL CONTACTS

BC FERRIES

FERRIES FROM THE MAINLAND to Vancouver Island. Consider making reservations to avoid a lengthy wait on summer weekends and holidays.

🌐 www.bcferries.com 📞 1-888-BC-FERRY (1-888-223-3779)

BC PARKS

PART OF THE PROVINCIAL Ministry of Environment, which protects some of the best representative elements of British Columbia's natural and cultural heritage. British Columbia's Protected Area system provides for the protection and maintenance of important natural and cultural values and outstanding outdoor recreation opportunities. See the website for updates, trail conditions, and visitor alerts.

🌐 www.bcparks.ca

BC TRANSIT

COMMUNITY BUS SERVICE ON the North Island.

🌐 www.bc.transit.com/regions/mtw   📞 250-956-3151

NORTH COAST TRAIL SHUTTLE LTD.

WATER TAXI AND LAND shuttle to and from the east and west ends of Cape Scott Provincial Park from Port Hardy.

🌐 www.capescottwatertaxi.ca
    www.northcoasttrailshuttle.com

📞 250-949-6541 / 1-800-246-0093

WATER TAXI

- At the time of writing, the minimum charge for the boat is $360 plus tax with a $90 per person rate when the minimum is met. There is a discount of $15 per person for groups of eight or more people.
- Departure is from the Quarterdeck Marina at 8:00 a.m. Arrive 30 minutes early to allow for parking and loading. Pick-up from Shushartie Bay is 9:00 a.m when booked (camping at the Shushartie Bay forest campsite will ensure that you don't miss the pick-up).
- Travel time is approximately 50–60 minutes.
- In addition to services to Shushartie Bay, the water taxi provides drop-off points along the coast, allowing for alternative start points that may help to shorten your hike.

SHUTTLE

- The shuttle van has a minimum charge of $225 plus tax or $75 per person when the minimum is met. The shuttle company tries to join smaller groups together to charge the lower, per-person rate. Discounts are available for groups of eight or more people.

Water taxi departs Shushartie Bay.

- Departure from Port Hardy is at 11 a.m. Pick-up time from the Cape Scott/San Josef Bay trailhead parking lot is between 1:00 pm and 2:00 p.m. (confirm with the shuttle company).
- Travel time from the parking lot to Port Hardy is approximately 1 hour and 45 minutes. This includes a 20-minute stop at the Scarlet Ibis pub in Holberg for a beverage and snack if desired.

FISHERIES AND OCEANS CANADA

PROVIDES TIDE CHARTS FOR printing ahead of your trip.

🌐 www.waterlevels.gc.ca

GREYHOUND

BUSES FROM VANCOUVER ISLAND and mainland towns to Port Hardy.

🌐 www.greyhound.ca   📞 1-800-661-TRIP (1-800-661-8747)

ISLANDLINKBUS

EXPRESS BUSES TO PORT Hardy from Nanaimo's Departure Bay ferry terminal and other Vancouver Island towns.

🌐 www.islandlinkbus.com

NORTH ISLAND DAYTRIPPERS

FULLY GUIDED DAYTRIPS WITHIN Cape Scott Provincial Park and other northwest coast areas.

🌐 www.northislandaytrippers.com   📞 1-800-956-2411

PACIFIC COASTAL AIRWAYS

FLIGHTS FROM VANCOUVER TO Port Hardy

🌐 www.pacific-coastal.com   📞 1-800-663-2872

PORT HARDY VISITOR CENTRE AND CHAMBER OF COMMERCE

🌐 www.porthardy.travel / www.ph-chamber.bc.ca
🏠 7250 Market St, Port Hardy
📞 250-949-7622 / 1-866-427-390

PORT MCNEILL VISITOR CENTRE

🌐 www.portmcneill.net 🏠 1594 Beach Dr, Port McNeill
📞 250-956-3131 / 1-888-956-3131

RECREATION TRAILS AND SITES IN BC

🌐 www.sitesandtrailsbc.ca

SAN JOSEF HERITAGE PARK PRIVATE CAMPGROUND AND BOAT LAUNCH

📞 250-288-3682

STRATEGIC NATURAL RESOURCE CONSULTANTS

PARK FACILITY OPERATOR FOR Cape Scott Provincial Park. Staff members are stationed throughout the park to carry out trail and facility maintenance. They are often available to provide assistance in case of an emergency.
🌐 www.snrc.ca 📞 250-956-2260

TOURISM BC

🌐 www.hellobc.com

VANCOUVER ISLAND NORTH

🌐 www.vancouverislandnorth.ca

APPENDIX 3
SUGGESTED ITINERARIES

THIS BOOK WAS WRITTEN assuming the user is hiking the North Coast Trail and Cape Scott as a single trip. However, there are several variations that allow for shorter trips, easier hiking, and even options to do an epic trip of nearly 100 km (62 mi). The following are some suggestions.

The distance of each suggested itinerary is cumulative, and includes round trip or out-and-back distance if relevant.

THE NORTH COAST TRAIL AND CAPE SCOTT
East to west. 7 days, 78.4 km (48.7 mi)

DOING THE TRAIL IN this order is a great way to save some of the most rewarding beaches of the park for last.
- DAY 1: Shushartie Bay to Skinner Creek.
- DAY 2: Skinner Creek to Cape Sutil.
- DAY 3: Cape Sutil to Irony Creek (Shuttleworth Bight).
- DAY 4: Irony Creek to Laura Creek.
- DAY 5: Laura Creek to Nels Bight.
- DAY 6: Day hike to explore Cape Scott lighthouse and area (second night at Nels Bight).
- DAY 7: Nels to Cape Scott/San Josef Bay trailhead.

- ALTERNATIVES:

  ADD A DAY and camp at Nissen Bight. Then, continue onto Nels Bight (or Guise Bay) for a night.

  ACCELERATE THE TRIP by hiking from Shushartie Bay to Nahwitti River, and from Irony Creek to Nissen Bight in one day.

CAPE SCOTT AND THE NORTH COAST TRAIL
West to east. 8 days, 78.4 km (48.7 mi)

GOOD FOR EXPERIENCED HIKERS who can pace themselves well. Allows for the more difficult (eastern) parts of the hike to be done with lighter bags.

- DAY 1: Cape Scott/San Josef Bay trailhead to Eric Lake (assumes a later arrival to the trailhead).
- DAY 2: Eric Lake to Nels Bight (alternatively, camp at Guise Bay or Experiment Bight).
- DAY 3: Day hike to explore Cape Scott lighthouse and area (second night at Nels Bight).
- DAY 4: Nels Bight to Laura Creek.
- DAY 5: Laura Creek to Irony Creek (Shuttleworth Bight). Alternatively, push on and camp at Wolftrack Beach (unofficial site).
- DAY 6: Irony Creek (Shuttleworth Bight) to Cape Sutil. Alternatively, push on to Nahwitti River.
- DAY 7: OPTION A: Cape Sutil to Skinner Creek.
  OPTION B: Nahwitti River to Shushartie Bay.
- DAY 8: OPTION A: Skinner Creek to Shushartie Bay (targeting water taxi pickup the next morning).
  OPTION B: Morning water taxi pick-up from Shushartie Bay.

NORTH COAST TRAIL "LIGHT"
4–5 days, 57.6 km (35.8 mi)

IF YOU'VE JUST GOT limited time but want to do the North Coast Trail, this is the hike for you.

· DAY 1–3 (OR 4): Follow the itineraries above, but skip Nels Bight and Cape Scott.

· DAY 4 (AND/OR 5): spend your last evening either at Shushartie Bay or, if you are hiking east to west, try to make time for a night at San Josef Bay, one of the most beautiful beaches in the park.

NORTH COAST TRAIL "LIGHT" HARD CORE
2 days, 57.6 km (35.8 mi)

SAME AS ABOVE, BUT faster. It has been done before. Good for you. But you don't need this book. It weighs too much, contains no calories, and has information you don't have time to look at. Recommended camping (or resting) at Irony Creek.

CAPE SCOTT LONG WEEKEND
3–4 days, 46.2 km (28.7 mi)

FOR THOSE WITH JUST a weekend or a little longer, the west side of the park has parking, easy, picturesque hiking, some of the best beaches, and fascinating history.

· DAY 1–2: From the Cape Scott/San Josef Bay trailhead, hike in to Nissen Bight, Nels Bight, or Guise Bay to set up base camp (if starting late, camp at Eric Lake and move to one of the above the next day).

· DAY 2: Day hike to Cape Scott lighthouse and back to base camp.

· DAY 3 OR 4: Depart back to the trailhead.

DAY HIKES

SAN JOSEF BAY
1–2 days, 5 km (3.1 mi) or more for exploring both bays.
A great introductory hike to the area for those looking for a beautiful backcountry destination without the gruelling terrain and long hikes. A great beginner's walk or family trip with a fantastic reward.

- DAY 1–2: Hike down to the beach and enjoy for as much time as you've got.

OTHER RECOMMENDED DAY HIKE DESTINATIONS
Eric Lake and Fisherman River

OTHER OPTIONS: WATER TAXI DROP-AND-GO

FOR THOSE TARGETING A specific beach or wanting to shorten the hike, the Cape Scott water taxi provides drop-off and pick-up. High tide is the ideal time for all stops. Confirm details with the water taxi operator. The following are some possible drop-off and pick-up points: Fisherman Bay (allows for an 8-hour ocean-view hike to/from Strandby River), Strandby River, Shushartie Bay, and between Skinner Creek and Nahwitti River.

APPENDIX 4

TRIP PLAN

PART OF BACKPACKING IS being self-sufficient and prepared. No one expects to get lost or injured, but the unexpected can occur. Before you hit the trail, fill out a trip plan and leave it with a friend or family member. Leaving a trip plan behind is one way to be a responsible outdoorsperson. Stick to the plan! In the event that you do not return as stated, your plan can be given to officials to help them find you.

Flight of the sandpipers. *Photo: Steve Fines*

HIKING PARTY DETAILS

NAME	AGE	GENDER	EXPERIENCE
1.			
2.			
3.			
4.			

MEDICAL CONDITIONS/ALLERGIES (IF APPLICABLE)

TRIP DETAILS

START POINT (TRAILHEAD)   DEPARTURE DATE/TIME

END POINT (TRAILHEAD)   RETURN DATE/TIME

ACCOMMODATIONS, INCLUDING DATES

TRIP ITINERARY (INCLUDING INTENDED CAMPSITES)

Day 1

Day 2

Day 3

Day 4

Day 5

Day 6

Day 7

Day 8

Day 9

TENT DESCRIPTION (BRAND/MODEL/COLOUR)

VEHICLE DESCRIPTION AND LICENCE PLATE

COMMUNICATION DEVICES AND NUMBERS

e.g. cell phone, satellite phone, VHS radio. Note that cell phones do not work in Cape Scott Provincial Park.

EMERGENCY CONTACTS

EMERGENCY CONTACTS FOR OTHER TRIP PARTICIPANTS

1.

2.

3.

4.

LOCAL CONTACTS

(e.g. transportation service providers, coast guard, Search and Rescue, police, etc.)

APPENDIX 5

UTM COORDINATES

THE FOLLOWING PROVIDES UTM coordinates for important features, mainly water sources, campsites, and beach access points. A few notes for reading the coordinates:

- Most, but not all, water sources labelled on the maps are listed here.

- UTM coordinates are rounded to 5 m and elevation to the nearest whole number. Beach access points do not list elevation (assumed to be at or near sea level).

- Coordinates are listed (and described) from the perspective of a hiker traveling from east to west.

- GPS coordinates use the UTM Zone 9N and NAD83 projection and datum.

	FEATURE TYPE	NORTHING (m North)	EASTING (m East)	ELEV. (m)	NOTES
	SHUSHARTIE BAY TO SKINNER CREEK (MAP 1)				
1	Water	5634795	573695	32	Running stream, good water source.
2	Campsite	5635210	572145	5	Skinner Creek campsite (located on the beach at the mouth of the creek).
	SKINNER CREEK TO CAPE SUTIL (MAP 2)				
3	Water	5634465	569595	11	Good water source at west side of Nahwitti River cable car crossing (about 3 hours from Skinner Creek).
4	Water	5635165	567940	30	Good water source on beach near the base of the Long Leg Hill stairs.
5	Water	5635560	566715	5	Main water source at Cape Sutil.
6	Beach access	5634780	571420	N/A	Steep beach access to forest from west Skinner Creek beach to Nahwitti River.
7	Beach access	5635250	568060	N/A	Beach access from forest following descent from Long Leg Hill stairs.
8	Beach access	5635160	567710	N/A	Access to beach from forest.
9	Beach access	5635230	567370	N/A	Access to beach from forest.
10	Beach access	5635425	566905	N/A	Access from forest to beach at east Cape Sutil.

	FEATURE TYPE	NORTHING (m North)	EASTING (m East)	ELEV. (m)	NOTES
CAPE SUTIL TO IRONY CREEK (SHUTTLEWORTH BIGHT) (MAP 3)					
11	Water	5635700	565015	2	A stream on the beach is accessible at low tide. Approximately 1 hour, 15 minutes west of Cape Sutil.
12	Water	5635575	564690	10	Good water source from a stream. Possibly seasonal. Approximately 1 hour, 45 minutes west of Cape Sutil.
13	Landmark	5635495	563650	5	Tombolo.
14	Water	5634735	563020	1	Seasonal creek leading out to the beach.
15	Water	5634625	562765	2	Water source coming out onto the beach. Quality is not great (looks boggy and murky), but you can follow it upstream if needed.
16	Campsite	5632850	561875	3	Irony Creek/Shuttleworth Bight.
17	Beach access	5635990	565985	N/A	Access from forest to beach. Potential camping on the rocky beach.
18	Beach access	5635820	565465	N/A	East side of third beach, on the route from Cape Sutil to Irony Creek (Shuttleworth Bight).
19	Beach access	5635815	565035	N/A	West side of third beach, on the route from Cape Sutil to Shuttleworth.
20	Beach access	5635600	563540	N/A	Access to forest from beach after tombolo.

	FEATURE TYPE	NORTHING (m North)	EASTING (m East)	ELEV. (m)	NOTES
	CAPE SUTIL TO IRONY CREEK (CONT.)				
21	Beach access	5634645	562565	N/A	Access to beach from forest.
22	Beach access	5633775	562005	N/A	Access from forest to last stretch of beach before Shuttleworth Bight. Mostly rocky beach.
	IRONY CREEK (SHUTTLEWORTH BIGHT) TO LAURA CREEK (MAP 4)				
23	Beach access	5632180	560630	N/A	Forest trail access from Shuttleworth Bight beach.
24	Beach access	5632015	557695	N/A	Following a series of pocket beaches, this is where the forest trail emerges for the last long stretch of beach hiking until Laura Creek.
25	Water	5632120	559940	2	Stream leading to Strandby River estuary.
26	Campsite (unofficial)	5632465	557930	3	Wolftrack Beach. Good camping on a sandy beach.
27	Water	5632075	557790	4	Located at the west side of the beach in a pile of driftwood. Possibly seasonal. Quality is decent, but could be followed upstream if needed
28	Water	5631710	556030	4	Stream coming out of salal, directly onto beach. Could be seasonal. About 1 hour west of Wolftrack Beach. Three other little streams in this area.

	FEATURE TYPE	NORTHING (m North)	EASTING (m East)	ELEV. (m)	NOTES
	IRONY CREEK TO LAURA CREEK (CONT.)				
29	Water	5631455	555485	3	A reliable stream creates a miniature waterfall as it falls from a pile of black rocks on the beach edge. Look for the coniferous tree with the bulbous roots.
30	Water (potential camping)	5630120	554745	15	Stream runs onto sand from the forest. Potential camping in the sandy area above high tide line if you have experience building a food locker.
31	Campsite	5628815	553620	7	Laura Creek campsite.
	LAURA CREEK TO NISSEN BIGHT (MAP 5)				
32	Water	5628250	552970	3	Good, consistent water source, 20 minutes west of Laura Creek. Stream emerges on the beach from beneath a jumble of driftwood.
33	Beach access	5628245	552850	N/A	Forest trail access on west side of Laura Creak beach.
34	Water	5627625	552055	11	Water source at boardwalk bridge. Good flow. Located within a boggier section of the trail.
35	Water	5627555	551985	12	Excellent water source. A second bridge is here at a larger creek crossing. A better source than nearby streams to the east. Marked by a whimsical miniature shelter atop a stump. Good rest/picnic area.

	FEATURE TYPE	NORTHING (m North)	EASTING (m East)	ELEV. (m)	NOTES
	LAURA CREEK TO NISSEN BIGHT (CONT.)				
36	Water	5627070	551835	18	River crossing (by foot). Excellent water source, runs year-round.
37	Water	5627915	549890	23	Water source at east side of Nissen Bight (about 100 steps from the forest trail lead down to the beach). Be careful not to pollute with food, dishwashing, or bathing as this pool is the only water source for Nissen Bight campers.
38	Campsite	5627230	549030	4	Nissen Bight beach and campsite.
	NISSEN BIGHT TO SAN JOSEF TRAILHEAD (MAPS 5 AND 7)				
39	Water	5621985	549005	11	Fisherman River. Excellent water source at river; close to campsite and outhouse.
40	Water	5619510	549510	20	Small creek, good flow.
41	Water	5618180	550960	26	St. Mary Creek, good strong running creek, north of Eric Lake campsite.
42	Campsite	5617005	551865	25	Eric Lake campsite.
43	Campsite	5613845	551180	12	San Josef Bay.

ACKNOWLEDGEMENTS

THE SUPPORT, GENEROSITY, AND encouragement of friends, family, and strangers made this project possible. I am indebted to many people whose kindness and assistance helped bring this book to completion.

Firstly, a big thank you to Harbour Publishing for taking on this project and for seeing it through to print. It is an honour to be published with you. Thank you to my editor Hazel Boydell and designers Mary White, Shed Simas, and Brianna Cerkiewicz for working back and forth on the draft to arrive at this finished product!

The people of the North Island provided extensive support and regional knowledge. Thank you for welcoming me to your communities and for your time answering questions and giving valuable guidance. In particular, I would like to thank Ruth Botel for historical information, photos, and feedback on the settlers of the Cape Scott area. I would also like to thank Chief Tom Nelson of the Quatsino First Nation, Juanita Johnston of the U'mista Cultural Centre, Jane Hutton of the Port Hardy Museum and Archives, and Randy Black of the Kwakiutl Band Council for facilitating a greater understanding of the history and the present-day significance of this special area. Thanks to Dave Trebett and Cathy Denham for recommendations, advice, and introductions to help make my time in Port Hardy as productive as possible.

A huge thank you to Strategic Forest Management, Cape Scott's Park Facility Operators. From the high-quality work inside the park, to all of the proactive "extras" they do to support Cape Scott's future, this company has been a true steward of the park. In particular, I wish to acknowledge David Wall and Shaun Korman. From the beginning, you've shared photos, mapping information, advice, helicopters, and a constant desire to support this project and help make it a success.

At BC Parks, I would like to thank Jim Gilliland and Jessie Moore for providing critical information, responding to my queries and for helping me track down information.

Thank you to my friends for taking precious time out of your personal lives to read the rough drafts and provide critical feedback to make it a more polished product. These generous hearts are Nina Fancy, Rowena Rae, Darcie Emerson, and Brian Springinotic.

The images in this book are courtesy of several talented photographers. Thank you to Andrew Bruce Lau, Steve Fines, Graham Smith, and David Akoubian for sharing your beautiful images. Please see page 231 for more information about these artists.

And finally, thank you to my friends and family, who have been my constant (and patient) allies and biggest champions—from babysitting to brainstorming and everything in between. Special thanks to Darcie, my right-hand woman, for offering unconditional kindness and facilitating the impossible, be it hiking in the Cape Scott rain with a broken arm or taking on the most important jobs while last-minute trips are underway. Dave, my mapper extraordinaire, for devoting countless hours, bottomless enthusiasm, and for being such a true friend on and off the trail. And last, but hardly least, to Aaron, for backing me from the beginning of this project, to the end, and everything in between—if this project were a backpack, you would certainly be my hip belt!

PHOTOGRAPHERS

STEVE FINES

⌂ Port Hardy, BC

🌐 www.natureone.ca

"I'm a self-taught photographer who has lived on north Vancouver Island for the past six years. My passion for photography stems from my love of nature; this is reflected in my work primarily being focused on landscapes and wildlife. With its raw pristine beauty, the North Island provides an endless supply of inspiration and photographic opportunities."

GRAHAM SMITH

⌂ Ottawa, ON

🌐 www.grahamksmith.com

"This remote and challenging trek offers endless opportunities for viewing wildlife. The highlight of my trip was watching a Vancouver Island wolf feeding in the early morning on the sandy beach at Shuttleworth Bight. It was an absolutely amazing scene that I won't soon forget, and also made carrying my not-so-practical camera gear well worthwhile."

DAVID AKOUBIAN

⌂ USA

🌐 www.bearwoodsphotography.com

ANDREW BRUCE LAU

⌂ Victoria, BC

Amateur photographer, aspiring chef, and hiking partner extraordinaire.

REFERENCES

CLIMATE DATA

Environment Canada. 2014. "Canadian Climate Normals 1971–2000."
http://www.climate.weatheroffice.gc.ca/climate_normals.

World Climate. 2010. "Cape Scott, BC, Canada: Climate, Global
Warming, and Daylight Charts and Data." http://www.
climate-charts.com/Locations/c/CN71111010313530.php.

HUMAN HISTORY & CULTURE

BC Ministry of Environment. 2008. "North Coast Trail Open to
Hikers." May 10. http://www2.news.gov.bc.ca/news_releas-
es_2005-2009/2008ENV0055-000740.htm.

BC Parks. 2008. Cape Scott Provincial Park Brochure Map.
http://www.env.gov.bc.ca/bcparks/explore/parkpgs/
cape_scott/capescott_brochuremap.pdf.

Botel, Ruth. 2000. "Cape Scott and Area." Map.

Botel, Ruth. 2011. Personal interview.

Francis, Daniel. 2000. "Shushartie Bay." *Encyclopedia of British
Columbia*. Madeira Park, BC: Harbour Publishing. http://
knowbc.com/limited/Books/Encyclopedia-of-BC/S/
Shushartie-Bay.

GeoBC. "BC Geographical Names." http://geobc.for.gov.bc.ca/
base-mapping/atlas/bcnames.

Galois, Robert. 1994. *Kwakwa̱ka'wakw Settlements, 1775 – 1920: A
Geographical Analysis and Gazeteer.* Vancouver: University of
British Columbia Press.

Howay, Frederic. 1941. *Voyages of the Columbia to the Northwest
Coast.* Boston: The Massachusetts Historical Society.

McKenna-McBride Royal Commission. 1916. *Report of the
Royal Commission on Indian Affairs for the Province of British
Columbia: Minutes of Decision 1913–1916.* Victoria, BC: Acme
Press Limited.

Nelson, Tom. 2011. Personal interview.

Nielson, Steffen Bohni. 2001. "Civilizing Kwakiutl: Contexts and
Contests of Kwakiutl Personhood, 1880 – 1999." PhD diss.,
University of Aarhus. http://www.hum.au.dk/ckulturf/
pages/publications/sbn/kwakiutl.pdf.

Sellers, Marki. 2003. "Negotiations for Control and Unlikely
Partnerships: Fort Rupert, 1849-1851." *British Columbia
Historical News*, 36.1:6–13.

Stooke, Philip. 1979. *Landmarks and Legends of the North Island:
A Trip by Foot, Boat and Memory around Northern Vancouver
Island.* London, ON: The University of Western Ontario.

Vancouver Maritime Museum. "*Beaver.*" Accessed June 26, 2012.
http://www.vancouvermaritimemuseum.com/page212.htm
(page removed).

Wavelength Magazine. 2012. "Cape Scott Provincial Park: North
Coast Trail." Map and pocket guide. Nanaimo, BC: Wild
Coast Publishing.

Wonders, Dr. Karen. "Kwakwa̱ka'wakw." http://www.firstna-
tions.de/fisheries/kwakwakawakw.htm.

PLANTS & ANIMALS

BC Parks. "Background Report." http://www.env.gov.bc.ca/ bcparks/planning/mgmtplns/capesctt/capebkgr.pdf.

Environmental Stewardship Division. 2003. *Cape Scott Provincial Park Management Plan*. Victoria, BC: Ministry of Water, Land and Air Protection. http://www.env.gov.bc.ca/ bcparks/planning/mgmtplns/capesctt/capescott_mp.pdf.

Environment Canada. N.d. "The Scott Islands: A Proposed Marine National Wildlife Area." http://www.ec.gc.ca/appa/default.asp?lang=En&n=90605DDB-1.

Innes, Tyler. 1996. "An ecosystem-based management approach for maintaining sandhill crane nesting habitat on northern Vancouver Island." Master's thesis, Royal Roads University. http://dspace.royalroads.ca/docs/bitstream/ handle/10170/357/Innes,%20Tyler.pdf?sequence=1.

Pasco, Juanita. 1998. *The Living World: Plants and Animals of the Kwakwaka'wakw*. Alert Bay, BC: U'mista Cultural Society.

Pojar, J., K. Klinka, and D.A. Demarchi. 1991. "Chapter 6: Coastal Western Hemlock Zone." *Ecosystems of British Columbia*. Special Report Series 6. Victoria, BC: BC Ministry of Forests. http://www.for.gov.bc.ca/hfd/pubs/Docs/ Srs/Srs06.pdf.

Royal Canadian Geographic Society. N.d. "Species: Bald Eagle." http://www.canadiangeographic.ca/ wildlife-nature/?path=english/species/bald-eagle.

U'mista Cultural Centre. "Preserving the Tradition of T'lina Making." http://www.virtualmuseum.ca/virtual-exhibits/ exhibit/preserving-the-tradition-of-tlina-making.

Vancouver Island Wilderness and Historical Conservation. "Roosevelt Elk." http://www.geog.uvic.ca/viwilds/iw-elk.html.

RECOMMENDED READING

BC Parks. 2014. Cape Scott Provincial Park website. http://
www.env.gov.bc.ca/bcparks/explore/parkpgs/cape_scott.

Boas, Frances. 1925. *Contributions to the Ethnology of the Kwakiutl*. Columbia University Contributions to Anthropology,
vol. 3, New York: Columbia University Press.

Curtis, Edward S. 1915. *The Kwakiutl*. The North American
Indian, vol. 10. Norwood, MA: Plimpton Press. http://curtis.
library.northwestern.edu.

Fisher, Robin. 1977. *Contact and Conflict: Indian-European Relations in British Columbia, 1774-1890*. Vancouver: University of
British Columbia Press.

Francis, Daniel. 2010. "Where Mountains Meet The Sea: A Coastal
History." *KnowBC Blog*. April 11. http://knowbc.com/Know
bc-Blog/Where-Mountains-Meet-The-Sea-A-Coastal-
History21.

Peterson, Lester Ray. 1985. *The Cape Scott Story*. Langley, BC:
Sunfire Publications.

U'mista Cultural Centre. "The Kwakwa̱ka̱'wakw." http://www.
umista.org/kwakwakawakw/index.php.

INDEX

Page numbers in **bold** indicate photographs or maps